EDUCATION AND LEADERSHIP
FOR THE
TWENTY-FIRST CENTURY

EDUCATION AND LEADERSHIP
FOR THE
TWENTY-FIRST CENTURY

Japan, America, and Britain

BENJAMIN C. DUKE

Foreword by Donald M. Stewart

New York
Westport, Connecticut
London

Library of Congress Cataloging-in-Publication Data

Duke, Benjamin C.
    Education and leadership for the twenty-first century : Japan, America,
and Britain / Benjamin C. Duke ; foreword by Donald M. Stewart.
        p.   cm.
    Includes bibliographical references and index.
    ISBN 0-275-93986-3 (alk. paper)
    1. Education, Secondary—Japan—Evaluation.   2. Education,
Secondary—United States—Evaluation.   3. Education, Secondary—Great
Britain—Evaluation.   4. Leadership.   I. Title.
LA1316.D85   1991
373.41—dc20   90-28074

British Library Cataloguing in Publication Data is available.

Library of Congress Catalog Card Number: 90-28074
ISBN: 0-275-93986-3

First published in 1991

Praeger Publishers, One Madison Avenue, New York, NY 10010
An imprint of Greenwood Publishing Group, Inc.

Printed in the United States of America

The paper used in this book complies with the
Permanent Paper Standard issued by the National
Information Standards Organization (Z39.48-1984).

10 9 8 7 6 5 4 3 2 1

CONTENTS

FOREWORD

Like many historical phenomena, leadership is paradoxical in nature. It is both a function of, and in part a determining factor in, the societal nature over which it exercises sway. The same can be said of education. What, how, and why we teach our young people is defined by, but also defines, our social, political, and economic condition.

Seen in this light, education, leadership, and society form part of an essential calculus—three dependent variables whose interaction creates our continuously changing world.

Throughout most of history, when individual polities (whether nations or city-states) lived in relative independence, or only regional interdependence, leadership evolved in a clear, culturally specific way. The last several centuries, which have witnessed the military and political ascendancy of Europe and then the United States, have resulted in a style of leadership that most Westerners would find natural or at least familiar, if not always admirable. However, as author Benjamin C. Duke asserts in this most interesting book, with the rise of Japan to the status of an economic leader at the threshold of the globally interdependent twenty-first century, the question of leadership takes on a new dimension for citizens of Western countries. Professor Duke contends, "For the first time in modern history Western countries that had maintained economic supremacy for centuries, enabling them to extend their cultural influence throughout the world setting the pattern for international intercourse, must deal with non-Western people, the Japanese, as equals. It is somewhat baffling to both sides as they increasingly share responsibility for global leadership."

Unlike some other historians and political scientists, in this volume Professor Duke not only gives education its due, but goes to the often overlooked core of education, the students themselves. His work investigates the attitudes and vision of those young people at some of the leading high schools in Japan, the United States, and Great Britain who, Professor Duke asserts, will most likely provide the leaders of these nations in the twenty-first century. It is interesting to feel a reverberation in this approach of the famous phrase by the great Duke of Wellington, Arthur Wellesley, that "the battle of Waterloo was won on the playing fields of Eton." A century-and-a-half later, Eton is also on Professor Duke's list of quality secondary institutions in Great Britain.

Professor Duke makes two important assumptions. The first is that England and the United States are the nations to represent the West given their historical roles over the past two centuries. The second is that the ladder to leadership for the majority of individuals who hold political and economic power in all three nations is an educational one: quality high schools followed by elite universities, both public and private. The sharpness in his focus allows him to come to a very interesting conclusion. While the process of reaching leadership positions is the same—a combination of academic achievement and sports in a nurturing educational environment—the leadership styles are quite contrasting. In the West, verbal and intellectual skills, as well as the ability to take decisive action in a very visible context, tend to be the characteristics of leadership. In Japan, a studied self-effacement and the ability to work behind the scenes to create consensus within the group for a given policy is the more predominant leadership model.

For Western educators, it is also interesting to note that this stylistic difference in Japan reflects a social norm that is reinforced by the style of education. Students are passive members of relatively large classes devoted to a noninteractive learning experience of absorbing important facts presented by teachers whom they respect, but with whom they have little other contact. By contrast, in the elite schools of Great Britain and the United States, students are part of small, very interactive classes where memorization and retention of factual information is often eclipsed by emphasis on the process of defining and presenting knowledge, and, especially in the secondary schools, teachers are in close contact with their students.

From this analysis, two questions immediately spring to mind. First, if in fact leadership will be shared among these three nations in the next century, are the two quite different styles of leadership compatible? Will it be possible to create a relatively stable global community given two different approaches?

Second, in view of the success of Japan in terms of economic strength, is the current Western approach to leadership still a viable one? Or will we have to change our mode of leadership, and thus of education, in order to remain competitive with our Eastern partner?

Notwithstanding the "outbreak of peace" that occurred during 1990, the outbreak of war that occurred at the beginning of 1991 tragically clouds the issue of leadership as it is considered in this volume. The assumption has been that the world's intensely interrelated economies, and the apparent triumph of capitalism in various forms, would mitigate against the use of military force and turn competitive energies to the economic sphere. If, unfortunately, that turns out not to be the case, then leadership will most likely revert to a style of command and discipline predicated on military strength, at least for the near term. And if history is a guide, the Western mode has proved effective in this arena.

If, however, peace does definitively break out, and the economic struggles are the dominant ones, then Western educators and leaders may have to step back and reexamine their assumptions. Granted, there are a number of significant differences between economic enterprise as practiced in Japan and in the United States and England. Therefore, to pin the reasons for recent Japanese economic success solely on leadership may not be warranted. Nonetheless, the success of such things as Japanese-run businesses even in the United States, the high quality of Japanese products, and the strength of Japan's currency could not have been achieved without effective leadership. It may be that although more than any other sector it has come up through the exact route which Professor Duke so clearly outlines here—quality secondary schools, elite universities, and graduate schools, with concentration on small classes, intellectual competition and visible individualistic decision making—U.S. corporate leadership must reexamine its styles and its formation. The comments Professor Duke makes on the Japanese ability to respect and manage feelings within the group will present a special challenge to American educators and corporate leaders given the racial and ethnic diversity of our population and the emerging role of women, as opposed to the homogeneous make-up of the Japanese workforce and the essentially male composition of all its leadership positions. Nonetheless, the success of the consensus-conscious leaders in the Japanese economic sphere is a model that cannot be overlooked.

Professor Duke's analysis may also lead to reconsideration by those American educators who have taken the Japanese to task for their orientation toward factual as opposed to interactive learning. One of the most interesting findings of Professor Duke's work is that, despite their fascination with Western music, clothing, and culture, Japanese students on the leadership track are content with their mode of learning and the traditional way in which leaders exert influence in Japan. If these young people do in fact emerge as Japanese leaders, the prospect of change would appear to be less likely.

In summary, it is clear that Professor Duke has opened up a very provocative avenue for analysis. The complexities of the world situation notwithstanding, should peace prevail as we enter the twenty-first century, and thus economic activity remain the dominant issue, Western nations and Western corporate executives will need to take seriously the Japanese style of low-keyed, consensus-based leadership. One possible outcome might be that the demands of global responsibility may necessitate some mutual modifications in leadership styles in order to insure compatible approaches in sharing global responsibilities. If this is the case, I think we may also see some modifications in the processes of education on both sides of the geopolitical aisle.

Donald M. Stewart
President, The College Board

ACKNOWLEDGMENTS

Since this book compares the outstanding schools in America, Britain, and Japan, it seems most appropriate to dedicate it to those figures, now deceased, commonly recognized as the "father of comparative education" in these three respective countries; and who played a unique role in my academic career preparing me to undertake such a research project that led to this book.

Joseph Lauwerys, Professor of Comparative Education, University of London. My first tutor in comparative education who introduced the field to me as a graduate student in his department, then considered the preeminent center for comparative education studies in the world under his tutelage; stimulated my interest in European education through his famous introductory course; and, upon his retirement, assigned me to his successor, Brian Holmes, to complete the doctorate in the field.

George Bereday, Professor of Comparative Education, Teachers College, Columbia University. Led me more deeply into the field of comparative education as a profession through his provocative courses at Teachers College, Columbia University, the American counterpart to London University; stimulated my students as a visiting lecturer in my courses in Japan; wrote the first definitive book in comparative education still in use in my undergraduate course; and introduced me to Lawrence Cremin, who presented the most inspiring and unforgettable courses on American education unknowingly preparing me for my present assignment as Director of American Studies at ICU.

Masunori Hiratsuka, Director, National Educational Research Institute, Tokyo. Introduced me to the problems of education in Japan from a comparative perspective; and lectured as my guest in my courses at International Christian University, demonstrating that this leading Japanese scholar in the field of comparative education could be every bit as stimulating, erudite, and witty in the classroom as his close friends and colleagues from the West, doctors Lauwerys and Bereday.

1

EDUCATION FOR LEADERSHIP

Divergent Patterns between East and West

With the twenty-first century relentlessly approaching, many of those destined for leadership during that era are currently enrolled in outstanding secondary schools around the globe. Although teenagers today, they will be governing tomorrow, forming national and international policies of enormous consequence. Strikingly different from the twentieth century, which dawned amidst the horse-and-buggy era, the twenty-first century begins without historical precedent in a world immersed in supercomputers, lasers, and nuclear missiles. Dubbed by pundits as the century of high technology, the new era presents challenges for our future leaders unimaginable to their predecessors.

If trends under way during the latter half of this century continue, a shift in terms of power and influence in international affairs will result in new patterns of global leadership and diplomacy in the next century. Britain and the United States, world leaders during the nineteenth and twentieth centuries respectively, are in differing stages of declining influence in the international order, most noticeable in finance and commerce. Although both countries, especially the United States with its military power as displayed in the Gulf War, will retain prominent roles in the twenty-first century, their once-dominant role in global affairs has been gradually diminished by the expanding influence of other nations.

Japan manifestly represents a nation on the rise. Ascending from the ashes of military defeat into an economic superpower within a few decades, the Japanese have become a people of extraordinary significance at the turn of the century. Although there are critics who differ, an impressive number of knowledgeable analysts predict that the pace of events already set in motion in Japan, as well as in America and Britain, will continue well into the twenty-first century. Regardless of the speculative controversy over the relative front-running positions, Japan's new status among the leading nations of the world must be reckoned with.

Within the shifting currents of international relationships, the quality of leadership emerging from countries that attain international prominence becomes of great importance. The capabilities of their leaders affect not only the home country. Indeed, their attitudes and perceptions assume universal significance. In a world interconnected by global communication networks, and interdependent through commercial patterns, their decisions affect us all.

What, then, can we anticipate from the twenty-first century leaders of Japan, many of whom are at this very writing studying in their country's outstanding high schools? Are they of the caliber of leaders befitting a nation of such global importance? What attitudes and perceptions do they have of themselves, their country, and other people in the world? How do they view the moral and ethical problems confronting not only their country but mankind as a whole? Do they face the future, in which they are destined to play a formidable role, with confidence? These are vital questions since substantial research indicates that general attitudes formed by the secondary school level are carried over into adulthood. In other words the current attitudes and perceptions held by outstanding high school students today, who will become tomorrow's leaders, indicate how the leadership class of the twenty-first century will conduct the affairs of human activity.

In order to more fully appreciate, and speculate about, the future leaders of Japan who will assume an expanded role in world affairs in the twenty-first century, we will analyze their perceptions from an international perspective. How do their attitudes compare with those of the future leaders of other countries who will share responsibility with the Japanese for making decisions that affect the progress of civilization? In particular, how do their attitudes compare with those held by the future leaders of Britain and America, also studying in the classrooms of outstanding schools, who come from societies that have experienced global leadership and who will continue to play a critical role in world affairs interacting with the future leaders from Japan?

This research was designed precisely to identify, and survey the attitudes and perceptions of, the future leaders of these three countries, Japan, America, and Britain. A variety of reasons underlie the specific selections. First of all, the three nations are representative of the "old world" of Europe, the "new world" of North America, and the center of modern Asia. Britain was chosen from the European sector since, as mentioned, it represented the most powerful country of the nineteenth century and retains considerable global influence, in part, as titular leader of the forty-nine-nation Commonwealth of former British colonies. America represents the most influential nation of the twentieth century and will assuredly carry much of that influence into the next century, especially in military affairs. And Japan, as the most recent economic super power, epitomizes a vital Asian force of enormous potential in the twenty-first century of high technology. In other words, the future leaders of these three countries from three separate areas of the world are destined to play a major role in both national and international affairs in the next century. Their attitudes about themselves, their country, and toward each other form the basis of this study, enabling us to speculate on the future prospects of Japanese leadership from a comparative perspective.

America, Britain, and Japan also maintain unique bilateral relations that bind them together in an international relationship that extends around the globe. In spite of the intimate ties between America and Britain just half a century ago against their common Asian foe, Japan, their contemporary interlocking relationships corporately render them political and ideological allies. Individually, they have become major industrial and financial competitors. We begin with a brief background of the bilateral Japanese-American relationship from which the attitudes of their future leaders toward each other have developed.

The longest-serving American ambassador to Japan, the Honorable Mike Mansfield, argued persuasively throughout his tenure that the paramount relationship in the world during the latter half of the twentieth century, bar none, is that between Japan and America. He predicted this unique relationship would continue well into, if not throughout, the twenty-first century. Most Japanese consider Ambassador Mansfield's evaluation as valid from their perspective. Many Americans find it a curious concept difficult to comprehend.

Japanese-American relations extend well back into the latter half of the 1800s. At that time Japan's seclusion policy from external influence, pursued by the Tokugawa government for several hundred years, finally crumbled under American pressure extending its fledgling power into East Asia. In the process of modernization and industrialization thereafter, America played a role model for the Japanese. They aggressively sought the secrets of westernization primarily from Americans thought to be endowed with enlightened qualities worthy of emulation.

Throughout the twentieth century, in war and peace, the United States exerted the dominant external influence on Japanese society and its institutions. Japanese students today cannot proceed through the school system without becoming aware of America's intimate relationship with, and influence on, Japan in the modern period. Conversely, American students have little knowledge or appreciation of their nation's profound historical ties with Japan in the prewar period. Their perception of Japan is primarily an outgrowth of the widespread availability of attractive Japanese products on the American consumer markets.

One of the most critical developments in this East-West relationship at the turn of the century concerns the reversal of roles between these two economic superpowers. The dominant financial and technical position of America throughout most of the twentieth century has been challenged by Japan as the twenty-first century approaches. The substantial annual trade imbalances in Japan's favor reflect only one powerful indication of the new role Japan plays in the international order. Inevitably ambivalent reactions have emerged within the United States toward Japan's newly gained status, challenging that of America, and the growth of Japanese influence in domestic affairs by rapidly expanding investments throughout the United States. Current events have thrust Japanese-American relations into the very center of concern in both countries. In particular, the American media and many of the political leaders increasingly envision the Japanese as unresponsive to American policies and interests in such areas as the violent Middle East.

In order to evaluate the long-range consequences of Japan's rising status vis-à-vis the United States, as that Asian nation assumes one of the leading financial and technical positions in the world, this study surveyed the attitudes of the future leaders of America toward the Japanese, and future Japanese leaders toward America. From that perspective, an assessment can be made of the future prospects in the bilateral relationship for the twenty-first century. The concern, though, is primarily with Japanese leadership as it deals with American leaders, long accustomed to view the world atop a powerful base, from Japan's expanded position of influence never attained before.

The attitudes of the leaders of the twenty-first century in Japan and the United States toward each other are of enormous significance not only to these two nations, however; they are of vital importance to the international community as well. As two of the major producing nations of the world, and the primary consumers of the world's natural resources, most notably oil, the state of their bilateral relations greatly influences the global community. The developing nations in particular not only share a vested interest in Japanese-American relationships, but their future welfare depends more than ever before on Japanese policies and the attitudes of their leaders. Simply stated, Japan has become the major donor of aid and assistance to the third world.

Anglo-Japanese relations are similarly unique. Britain, although located on the far side of the globe from Japan, has traditionally played a unique role in modern Japanese history. When the Meiji government in the 1870s and 1880s sought models from the Western world to modernize Japanese society and industry, their emissaries were dispatched not only to America but also to Europe, including Britain. There they gained invaluable knowledge about many aspects of modern technology, such as naval advancements from the powerful British navy then ruling the waves. Even prior to the official opening of Japan to the West, England attracted the daring Japanese. For example, Mori Arinori, father of the modern Japanese school system, was secretly smuggled out of Japan in 1865 at the age of eighteen on a ship to England, where he began his Western studies. He later became the ambassador from Japan to the powerful Court of St. James.

During more recent times following World War II, Britain continued its distinct relationship with Japan throughout the American period. Because of America's location, its leadership in twentieth-century world affairs, and its victorious armies over Japan in the Pacific War, the U.S.-Japanese relationship justifiably dominated Japan's foreign policy. Nevertheless Britain continued its consistently warm relations with the Japanese, many of whom harbor a special feeling toward venerable British institutions such as the royal family and the medieval universities. As with American youth, few British teenagers are aware of the indispensable role their country played in Japan's history during both the early and modern periods. Likewise, few Japanese youth appreciate or comprehend the important contributions the British made to the modernization of Japan.

Anglo-Japanese relations during the decade of the 1980s have taken on an even greater urgency than before. With the rise of Japan as an economic superpower in such a brief period propelling that nation into the center of global affairs, Japanese leaders have looked beyond their preeminent ties with the United States to Britain as perhaps their second most important relationship in the West. Anticipating the formation of an integrated Europe in 1992, Japanese investments in the United Kingdom have been substantially increased, with over 100 Japanese companies producing goods within its borders. The Japanese presence in the financial markets of London, one of the world's leading financial centers, has multiplied virtually exponentially during the 1980s. It would appear that Britain has been targeted for further investments for Japanese participation not only in Britain's development, but also in the European Community, the world's largest unified market with well over 300 million residents within one economic boundary.

In an address given at this writer's university in Tokyo, the British ambassador characterized contemporary Anglo-Japanese relations as "good as they have ever been historically." With Britain's participation in the integrated European Community, this comforting bilateral relationship will assume much more vitality at the turn of the century. By that time, the world may be more clearly divided into several major regional trading groupings including North America, the European Community, the Pacific area led by Japan, and the Soviet Union's remaining sphere of influence.

With Japan relying more than ever before on smooth relations with

Britain, given the fact that it seeks to expand its markets within the powerful new European partnership, British attitudes toward the Japanese assume an even greater urgency to them. Although the British ambassador stated unequivocally that "there are virtually no problems at all regarding Japanese investments in the United Kingdom," the acutely sensitive Japanese never feel completely assured of their welcome. For example, only a few perceptive Americans or Japanese would have anticipated just a decade ago the backlash toward Japanese investments in the United States emerging today.

In the not-too-distant future of the twenty-first century, Anglo-Japanese relations will assume major importance in world affairs. Britain, as the largest overseas investor by far among the European Community, and Japan, the rapidly expanding global investor with 30% of its EC investments already in the United Kingdom, may develop mutually beneficial or antagonist relationships. Either way the pendulum swings, the results will extend far beyond purely bilateral interests. In order to gain some insights into the future relationships between Japan and Britain, and the long-range consequences of Japan's expanding investments in the United Kingdom and into the European Community, this study was also designed to survey the attitudes of the future leaders of Britain toward Japan and the Japanese, and future Japanese leaders toward Britain and the British. In the process the assessment of the capability of Japan's future relations vis-à-vis an integrated Europe can also be undertaken as Japan's influence extends well beyond its traditionally strong American ties.

Finally, although this analysis places primary emphasis on the future leaders emerging from Japan, and their attitudes toward themselves, their country, and America and Britain, the Anglo-American relationship is also considered. These ties extend, of course, from the very beginning of America as a land of diverse British colonies. The so-called special relationship has continued ever since, through war and peace. As two nations sharing a common heritage, language, religion, and political perspective, the bilateral relationship fits the description of allies most comfortably, surviving all strains in the past.

Within this general framework of international relationships, then, our purpose is to attempt to assess how the prospective leaders of Japan will respond to the challenges they face in world affairs as the first and only superpower from Asia in modern history. But no analysis of a nation's leadership potential can be undertaken without considering the schools, their goals and purposes, and the general educational milieu from which the future leaders originate. This pursuit inescapably leads us to the very heart of a nation's tradition, culture, and codes of conduct. They are all inextricably woven into a nation's leadership capabilities.

An assumption underlying this research is that many of the individuals destined to assume twenty-first-century leadership positions are currently studying at the most outstanding secondary schools in their respective countries. Although leaders also arise from ordinary schools, the contention is that the outstanding schools in every nation produce a disproportionate share of graduates who enter the better universities. This places them in a decidedly more advantageous position to eventually enter the leadership class in most sectors of the society. Thus many of the students enrolled in outstanding secondary schools today will hold positions of influence in determining American, British, and Japanese policy in the future, including the formation of domestic, bilateral, and global relationships.

Concerning attitudes and attitudinal changes, especially in the realm of political socialization, research shows that early experiences are "the crucial factor in determining political orientation"; that an "individual's attitudes and beliefs have already, to a large extent, taken firm root by the time he is consciously aware of politics," which takes place by about the mid-teens. Consequently when the individual passes through secondary school, his or her "basic political orientations to regime and community have become quite firmly entrenched." Further studies reveal that little change takes place in attitudes during that period, remaining fairly stable throughout adulthood.[1]

Therefore, if the current attitudes toward each other held by students studying at the outstanding schools in America, Britain, and Japan are positive, then the future relationships between these nations closely allied today should rest on a sound basis as these students enter the leadership classes of tomorrow. Conversely, if their attitudes toward each other are negative today, this could signal a highly critical shift in future relations that would have an adverse influence on world affairs. In other words, from the contemporary attitudes of students in the outstanding secondary schools in America, Britain, and Japan today, we can anticipate the state of relations, both international and bilateral, that will unfold during the twenty-first century.

Beyond that, by studying the current attitudes and perceptions of the outstanding students of Japan, in comparison to their Western counterparts, we can also speculate knowledgeably about the type of leadership that will emerge from Japan within the not-too-distant future. By drawing a profile of Japan's outstanding students today, in the context of their outstanding schools, we can predict to some degree the very quality of Japan's leaders for tomorrow.

In order to select secondary schools representative of the rather select category of "outstanding," that is, those schools, both public and private, that are producing more than their share of future leaders nationally and regionally, a different approach was taken in each country. The American selection proved more complex because of the size of the country as well as the diversity of its schools. However, perhaps contrary to the image most Americans have of their leadership class, the selection of schools from the private sector was much more accommodating than originally envisioned.

As one study describes it, "Great power in America is concentrated in a tiny handful of people. A few thousand individuals . . . decide about war and peace, wages and prices, consumption and investment, employment and production, law and justice, taxes and benefits, education and learning, health and welfare, advertising and communication, life and leisure. In all societies—democratic, capitalist or socialist—only a few people exercise great power."[2]

More precisely, the same researcher painstakingly counted the top institutional positions of leadership in America, arriving at a figure of exactly 7,314 that, taken collectively:

control half of the nation's industrial assets: half of all assets in communication, transportation and utilities; half of all banking assets; two-thirds of all insurance assets; and they direct Wall Street's largest firms. They control the television networks, the influential news agencies, and the major newspaper chains. They control nearly 40 percent of all private university foundations. They direct the nation's largest and best-known New York and Washington law firms as well as the nation's major civic and cultural organizations. They occupy key federal government positions in the executive, legislative and judicial branches. And they occupy all the top command positions in the Army, Navy, Air Force and Marines.[3]

Nearly all of the top leaders of America hold university or college degrees, with 54% of corporate leaders and 42% of government leaders graduating from just twelve heavily endowed, prestigious private universities, notably within the Ivy League. A poll taken at the beginning of this decade of chief executive officers of Fortune 500 companies showed that "Yale tops all schools in its share of alumni CEOs, with Princeton a strong second, followed by Harvard."[4] Furthermore, it is estimated that up to 20% of corporate leaders and 10% of government leaders are graduates of only thirty-three private preparatory schools, many with profound historical ties to the Ivy League universities.[5] Four of these thirty-three schools, it should be noted, are included in this study.

To select representative outstanding secondary schools in the United States, admissions officers of twenty of the leading universities and colleges throughout America were asked to list five private and five public secondary schools considered by them as outstanding based on their experiences in student admissions. Fifteen complied. In addition, various well-known individuals most knowledgeable about American education, such as Dr. Theodore Sizer, former dean of the Harvard Graduate School of Education, were also invited to suggest outstanding American secondary schools based on their unique experiences. Finally, in one instance only, the Bureau of Educational Research of a representative state was asked to submit the names of four of the most outstanding high schools in that state, from which one was chosen for the survey.

From a master list compiled from the many individual lists, plus the one school chosen from the four recommended at the state level, a final selection of sixteen of the most outstanding schools in the United States was made. The participating schools reflect both the public and private sectors and, insofar as possible, geographical diversity. A number of the well-known private boarding schools in New England were included where the role of the school in preparing the future leaders of America is emphasized. Their special role in educating significant numbers of American leaders, referred to previously, underlies the decision to include a disproportionate number of them even though a small minority of American high school students are enrolled in these prestigious private schools.

The public sector is also solidly represented in this study by nationally renowned high schools from the north, south, east, central, and western United States, in some cases where the sciences prevail with representation of future leaders in the technological and scientific fields. Regionally well-known public schools were also chosen so that a broad cross-section of future leaders, not just at the national level, could participate in the survey. Overall, the schools listed in Table 1 are considered representative

Table 1
Participating American schools

Private	Public
Andover (Mass.)	Cherry Creek (Col.)
Brearly School for Girls (N.Y.)	Highland (Tex.)
Choate (Conn.)	New Trier (Ill.)
Collegiate (N.Y.)	North Carolina High
Harvard (Cal.)	School of Science
Hotchkiss (Conn.)	and Mathematics
Pine Crest (Fla.)	Palo Alto (Cal.)
Westminster (Ga.)	Parkway (Mo.)
	Radnor (Pa.)
	Stuyvesant (N.Y.)

of the most outstanding private and public secondary schools in the United States, educating many of America's future leaders for the twenty-first century.

In order to select appropriate British schools for this study, both public and private, many knowledgeable people were consulted. The inquiry began with British Council representatives in Tokyo. That was followed by extensive consultations in the United Kingdom with representatives from both the private and public sectors and at the local and national levels, including the Department of Education and Science. University scholars well-versed on issues in British education were also consulted.

The private sector, notably the so-called British Public Schools, with its historical role of educating impressive numbers of British leaders via Oxford and Cambridge Universities, was given a prominent position in this project. Way back in 1867, the Taunton Commission identified seven of these private schools—Eton, Harrow, Winchester, Westminster, Charterhouse, Rugby, and Shrewsbury—as the major schools educating the top classes of British students at that time.

A contemporary author summarizes succinctly their current role accordingly: "The fact that over 100 years later these same seven schools, along with later additions to the still loosely defined public schools, continued to attract such a high level of public interest reinforces the . . . view that they form a point of reference for the whole British education system defining the norms and values from which all other strata flow."[6] Another author contends unequivocally that "the public schools continue to play a dominant role in the self-perpetuation of recruitment to elite positions in Britain."[7]

Although there are many private schools in England, these and other authors are, when referring to the "public schools," distinguishing them as members of the Headmaster's Conference of private fee-paying schools. Accordingly, eight of the schools in this study (see Table 2) are from that very select group. Furthermore, four of our eight are among the original seven schools on the famous list drawn up by the Taunton Commission of 1867 as the most outstanding schools in the land at that time.

The procedure for selecting outstanding secondary schools that graduate more than their share of future leaders in Japan was straightforward. Due to the hierarchical structure of the Japanese educational system, the most prominent universities are commonly recognized, beginning with the national universities of Tokyo and Kyoto and the private universities of Keio and Waseda. The precise number of secondary school graduates who enter these prestigious institutions, leading to the top positions in virtually all sectors of the society, is published each year listing the names of those schools in order of entering graduates. That list, heavily influenced by Tokyo University, in effect establishes an unofficial classifica-

Table 2
Participating British schools

Private	Public
Charterhouse	Blue Coat (Comprehensive);
Eton	Liverpool
Harrow	City of Stroke-on-Trent
Manchester Grammar	(Sixth Form College);
Merchant Taylor's	Staffordshire
Royal Grammar	London Oratory (Comprehensive)
Rugby	Ward Freeman (Comprehensive);
St. Paul's	Hertfordshire

tion of high schools throughout the land in the minds of the Japanese public. It permeates the educational establishment.

In order to more fully appreciate the position of Japan's leading universities, into which the outstanding high schools place a disproportionate number of their graduates on the ladder to leadership, pertinent statistical tables are included below. According to a poll taken by the business magazine *Diamond Shukan*, of the 35,517 executive officers of Japan's leading corporations in every sector, four universities stand out among the 224 ranked institutions as shown in Table 3.[8] Following that, data is presented concerning the number of members sitting in the lower house of Japan's parliament, where political power lies, according to their university degree (Table 4).[9]

By incorporating the list of high schools placing the highest number of students in the most famous national universities with those that feed into the distinguished private universities, along with several from the more local but well-known universities, supplemented by the annual lists of successful applicants on the national examination for first-rank government positions, a final selection of Japan's outstanding schools was made. In addition, insofar as was reasonable, schools located outside the Tokyo metropolitan area, where the greatest concentration of outstanding schools is located, were also included. Finally, Japanese specialists most knowledgeable about domestic educational affairs were consulted before a final list of institutions representative of the most outstanding Japanese secondary schools educating more than their share of leaders was drawn up. Following Japanese fashion, the final composition was noticeably

Table 3
Graduates from the major universities of executive officers among Japan's leading corporations

- Total of 35,517 -

Rank Order	Graduates	Total Enrollment
1. Tokyo University	4,491	14,000
2. Waseda University	2,590	42,000
3. Keio University	2,421	23,000
4. Kyoto University	2,134	11,000

Graduates in the

financial sector only

- Total of 1849 -

Rank Order	Graduates
1. Tokyo University	391
2. Keio University	167
3. Kyoto University	128
4. Waseda University	102

Graduates in the

chemical sector only

- Total of 1,936 -

Rank Order	Graduates
1. Tokyo University	315
2. Kyoto University	208
3. Keio University	131
4. Waseda University	128

influenced by Tokyo University. Ten of our schools (Table 5) rank among the top twenty high schools placing the greatest number of their graduates into that university, including the top two, Kaisei and Nada, which each average the astonishing rate of nearly 140 per year.

Table 4
Lower House Diet members according to university degrees

Lower House Diet members

according to university degrees

- Total of 512 -

Rank Order	Graduates
1. Tokyo University	101
2. Waseda University	62
3. Keio University	42
4. Kyoto University	13

Table 5
Participating Japanese schools

Private	Public
Azabu (Tokyo)	Chiba
Kaisei (Tokyo)	Kunitachi (Tokyo)
Lasalle (Kagoshima)	Urawa (Saitama)
Oiin Girls (Tokyo)	Sendai First
Nada (Kobe)	Shuyukan (Fukuoka)
Rakusei (Kyoto)	Tsukuba (Tokyo)

The forty schools participating in this project are considered, then, as representative of the most outstanding secondary schools in America, Britain, and Japan. Several private schools on the list are recognizable as world-renowned. As indicated previously, an attempt was made to include appropriate representatives from both the private and public sectors commensurate with the roles they play in their respective nations. Coeducational schools as well as girls' schools were also included wherever possible. Finally, a few outstanding regional schools, in contrast to the nationally and even internationally famous schools, were invited to participate on the grounds that these institutions are graduating more than their share of regional leaders.

In order to render the samples comparable, and sufficient in size to be meaningful, over 1,000 senior students per country participated in this survey. Choosing older students around eighteen years of age implied the

Table 6
Participating students

Participating students

	Private	Public	Total
America	501	620	1,121
Britain	760	340	1,100
Japan	492	574	1,066

highest level of maturity, experience, and sophistication in dealing with the substantive questions in the survey. Each school, then, arranged to have between 60 and 100 senior students, including a fairly equal number of males and females in coeducational schools, participate so that a minimum number of 1,000 samples per country became available. The number of students per school depended somewhat on the relative size of the school and the total number of schools per country. Well over 3,000 of the most outstanding students in America, Britain, and Japan were ultimately involved in this study (Table 6).

A comprehensive questionnaire was carefully constructed to survey the 3,000-plus participants about their attitudes and perceptions toward themselves, their country, each other, and the future. A special set of questions was also designed to survey the attitudes of all three groups toward American, British, and Japanese products and trading practices. The major irritant in U.S.-Japanese and Anglo-Japanese bilateral relations concerns the imbalances in international trade overwhelmingly in Japan's favor. It was deemed important, therefore, that the attitudes toward this most contentious issue between these countries by the future leaders of all three nations be given special consideration.

In nearly every instance, the identical questionnaire was completed by all three nationalities with only the names of the appropriate country inserted to fit the proper situation. A translation of the questionnaire into Japanese was made by competent university translators. A concerted effort was undertaken to reflect as accurately as possible the intent of the original version in English.

The survey was conducted in each country over a two-year period including the 1988-89 and 1989-90 academic years. The length of the project was purposely set for this period to avoid insofar as possible the potentially distorting influence of the American presidential election and the succession of Japanese prime ministers. It was also extended over a two-year period to more accurately gauge longer-term trends in attitudes of the Americans and British toward Japan's ongoing favorable balances of trade with them and the continuing accumulation of large real estate portfolios by the Japanese in America and, to a lesser extent, Britain.

The final stage of the study, follow-up interviews of senior students, was conducted during the calendar year 1990 in each of the three countries. Students from among the participating schools were interviewed either on a one-to-one basis or in small groups of two or three students each. The statistical results from the questionnaire of the respective country were presented to each student during the interviews. Student reaction to and analysis of the results were then solicited and discussed in an attempt to adequately interpret the data. In addition, a determination was made if general attitudes had undergone any significant changes from the time the questionnaires were completed. Although the questionnaires and interviews extended into the period of the monumental events in Eastern Europe, the data was collected prior to the ensuing crisis in the Middle East.

The interviews conducted in all three countries convincingly demonstrated that the students who participated in this survey, many of whom will become leaders in their countries in the twenty-first century, represent the most outstanding teenagers in America, Britain, and Japan today. In their own unique manner, their sophistication and level of awareness confirmed that these were not average high school students from typical families. No attempt, however, was made through the questionnaire to determine family background or social status, no matter how interesting that would be, since it was considered outside the original purpose of the study as well as unwieldly and somewhat sensitive to ascertain. It was a topic of the interviews, though. Clearly many of our students come from families of financial means since over half the representation is enrolled in private schools where fees and other costs are substantial, prohibitively so in many cases. The interviews reinforced this assessment.

The outstanding secondary schools in America and Britain only can be divided essentially into two categories, public and private, according to the vast differences between their physical facilities, general atmosphere, and tradition, among other factors. In Japan the distinction between the two sectors is far less evident. The outstanding Japanese public and private schools bear a strong mutual resemblance in facilities, classroom atmosphere, teaching methods, and tradition. Furthermore, they do not appear from the outside that much different from ordinary high schools.

In comparing the outstanding schools from all three countries, where many of their future leaders are currently enrolled, perhaps the most significant difference is evident between both the public and private Japanese schools and the public and private schools in America and Britain; that is, between East and West. What distinguishes the education of the

future leaders of these three countries most significantly are the differences in the outstanding Japanese schools from those in America and Britain. This includes, among others, school facilities, the relationship
between student and teacher in the classroom, and the general approach
to the education of the future leaders of their respective countries.

In spite of the vast differences between East and West, there is a singleness of purpose that unites them all regardless of nationality; namely, the
successful entry into the most prestigious universities of the land by as
many graduates as possible. In all three nations the category of outstanding secondary schools is based primarily on the degree of success the
individual school achieves in attaining the overriding goal of university
preparation. The school's reputation, and consequent desirability to
potential students and their parents, depends to a very great extent on
those annual figures of university entrance—not, it must be understood,
into ordinary universities. The secondary schools that can be classified as
outstanding in all three countries are those that continually send
significant numbers of their graduates into the leading universities,
notably at the national level and then regionally. Because of the sheer
physical size of the United States in comparison to Japan and Britain,
leading regional universities play an important role in establishing the
reputation of the secondary schools in their areas of influence.

As one student put it succinctly during an interview, "We are all well
aware of our privileged position." This declaration, implicitly understood
by many of our 3,000 participants regardless of the phrasing, describes
the situation appropriately. These students are part of a concentrated
effort by the school, its teachers and adminstrators, and the parents to
prepare them to pass the university entrance examination in its various
forms leading to the better universities. And this route, ultimately, leads
to positions of influence and success in most areas of their respective
societies for many of their graduates. That singleness of purpose has
become perhaps the primary reason for the very existence of the outstanding schools in this survey.

In America and Britain, many of the participating private schools take
pride in an educational tradition that extends several hundred years in the
past, even longer in the case of Britain. These are venerable institutions
that have acquired large endowments in land and/or funds enabling them
to provide facilities rivaling well-endowed universities. They comprise
large campuses with literally dozens of fine buildings, including a mixture
of older ornate structures and others of modern impressive design and
architecture. In both countries the exquisite rural sites of many of these
private institutions provide an educational environment so pristine and
yet so elaborate they defy comprehension by the Japanese.

One example is convincing proof not only of the elaborate facilities
available to the Western private student in our survey, but it also stands in

shocking contrast to the best-equipped private school in Japan. One private American school boasts the astonishing number of eighty separate buildings on campus, including completely independent facilities for art, English, science, psychology, music, mathematics, classics, history, and modern languages. There are, in addition, a communications center, a chapel, a three-story library, an archaeological museum, an alumni house, an inn, and a hockey rink, among other facilities. Sprinkled throughout are nearly fifty so-called houses where students live in closely monitored dormitory arrangements in one- or two-bed student rooms. There are similar private schools in Britain, one of which owns huge tracts of valuable playing grounds that run on and on. Student fees naturally reflect the costs of maintaining such an educational environment, thereby exerting a selective feature in student enrollments.

These elaborate private outstanding schools in America and Britain are not only inconceivable to the Japanese, they are unimaginable to many of their own people. The American public in particular is largely unaware of the scale of the facilities of a substantial number of their outstanding private schools, where far more than their share of graduates have gone on to take leadership positions throughout American society and industry. Few American public school teachers or students, for example, realize the extent of the differences between the physical environment in which they teach and that in a substantial number of the outstanding private schools in the United States.

Although the outstanding public schools in this study lack the accouterments of many of the private schools, such as venerable well-stocked libraries that rival small college libraries, extensive hockey and cricket pitches in Britain, or, in the case of a number of the New England private schools, ice hockey rinks, they are nevertheless well-ordered institutions. Some of them have good libraries and science facilities, while a few are still housed in unimpressive surroundings with little space for sports activities. In spite of the limitations in facilities, they exude a seriousness of purpose that rivals their private school competitors. And they are indeed competing for the outstanding students in the country regardless of their lack of the spacious facilities, venerable traditions, and boarding provisions that surround many of our private school participants. There is in virtually all of them a highly competitive atmosphere of academic excellence.

The outstanding private secondary schools of Japan producing more than their share of future leaders stand in sharp contrast to their Western counterparts. Because of the stark limitations of space in this tiny over-crowded land, rare is the private school located on a spacious campus in a secluded area, as are a significant number of our outstanding private American and British schools. Most outstanding Japanese private schools are crowded into metropolitan areas. Few have much more than the basic classroom building or two, a gymnasium, perhaps an administrative building, a few tennis courts, and, if fortunate, a separate building for science classes. Extensive sports fields or substantial library holdings, let alone an individual building to house the library books or science facilities, are seldom available. Limited dormitory facilities are available in a few private schools.

In contrast to the small classes of the Western private schools in our study, where ten to fifteen students per class is standard, Japanese classes are large in virtually all private schools. In the most prestigious private secondary schools in the land, the average class includes anywhere from fifty to fifty-five students in one classroom for the lesson. The desks necessarily must be placed in an orderly fashion, that is, in straight rows to accommodate the large number of students in one standard classroom.

With fifty or more students in a Japanese classroom in the major private schools, versus fifteen more or less in American and British private school classrooms, the relationship between the teacher and his or her outstanding students assumes a startlingly different character. There is a strong sense of community life with an informal, fairly close relationship between teacher and student at the American and British private schools. On the other hand the typical Japanese teacher in both our private and public schools formally lectures from prepared notes or the textbook for virtually the entire period. Few, if any, questions by either the serious teacher or the students interrupt the lecture routine. Busily taking copious notes, the students in Japan's outstanding schools expect nothing less than a teacher adept in preparing them for the most prestigious universities. If this means the dissemination of factual information most likely to be included in the university entrance examination for pure rote memorization, so much the better.

There are some teachers in a few of our Japanese schools who encourage student participation by asking questions and conducting a discussion among the class members. They are in a minority. In some of the classes where students participate, they become involved in an analysis of the finer points of issues that just may appear in the entrance examination. Speculation, opposing opinions, random thoughts, provocative opinions, and so on, are simply not part of the classroom routine in Japan, whether it be in the private or public sector. This is not to imply that the future leaders of Japan are sitting straight in their seats listening intently to the lecture while taking copious notes. In many instances this is not the case. There can be a considerable amount of private jibbering during the class, distracting at times. But everyone in the room has the same purpose in being there, and when the time comes for serious study, it takes place. Teachers can expect students to act accordingly. They do not have to be told. It is their decision to make.

One of the most notable features of these outstanding private Japanese secondary schools is their proven performance in covering the entire three-year mandatory national curriculum of core courses, set by the Ministry of Education, in a much shorter period. It is not uncommon for the very elite schools to complete the required course in two years or even less, devoting the remaining time of the three years to continuous review. That pace also enables them to go well beyond the national requirements. Consequently the most famous Japanese private schools that can be classified as outstanding in the hierarchical structure of the system provide their students that special edge over rival schools that fail to maintain such an intense pace in the all-encompassing competition for selection to the most famous universities. These, in turn, provide entree to the leading positions in government, industry, business, and the professions of Japan, as we have seen.

There are few distinguishing differences between the outstanding private and public secondary schools in Japan. The facilities are fairly standard. The number of students, large in both cases, may be just slightly lower in the public school classrooms, for example, forty-eight to fifty. The singleness of purpose, entry of as many graduates into the major universities, is common to them both. Consequently the classroom atmosphere is similar, although most public schools are coeducational. The major difference is that the private schools are currently attracting a higher percentage of the most capable students, thereby enabling them to place a greater percentage of their graduates into the highly selective universities. This cycle tends to feed itself. As a Japanese student from one of the most elite high schools analyzed it, "Our class was made up of all number-one students."

The American and British students enrolled in our outstanding private schools under review experience a diametrically opposite educational environment from the Japanese student. Not only are the physical facilities in most instances far more elaborate, and downright luxurious in comparison, the number of students in each class is ludicrously small. It is not uncommon in both America and Britain to find private school classes with ten or so students. In some schools, classes with as many as twenty students are considered exceptionally large. Even in the outstanding public schools in both America and England, class size remains thirty-five or under; many of the senior classes are smaller. In virtually all Japanese classrooms, private or public, from the first to the last year, the teacher will be faced with around fifty students.

With small groupings of students studying under one teacher, the relationship between student and teacher in the American and British classrooms can obviously produce a different character than the Japanese classroom. Depending upon the teacher, of course, there is much more give-and-take, question-and-answer, exchange of opinion, discussion, probing, and so on, in the small private school classrooms in America and Britain that would simply defy the imagination of their Japanese counterparts. Perhaps the atmosphere can best be described as relaxed but de-manding, as one student put it, where the underlying but certainly common purpose among students and teachers is the same as that in Japan: successful entry into the most select universities for as many graduates as possible. This writer well remembers a classroom visit to a leading American private coeducational boarding school class in which the history teacher announced to the twelve students that an exam review would be held in the teacher's apartment on Sunday evening, after they had dinner together. Although this is certainly not a common practice in these schools, it would be unthinkable in our Japanese schools.

From the learning point of view, the classrooms in America and Britain in our study can best be described as academically challenging. This description includes our outstanding public schools as well, where these students and their teachers are undergoing preparation for the same examinations as those in the private sector. Although the number of stu-dents in our public school classrooms is higher, more than double that of the private sector, there is also a much stronger effort to encourage the student to participate in the lesson than found in either the public or private classroom in Japan where some critics would describe it as essen-tially nonexistent. As an American student from the public sector recalled, "You never know when you're going to have a question fired at you." Few Japanese students share that anxiety.

One of the major characteristics of the outstanding Western schools in this study, although their preeminent academic mission is clear, comes through their efforts to treat the students as individuals with unique talents but limitations as well; to challenge the students to the limit of their ability; to encourage the students to think independently; to moti-vate the students to broaden personal interests; and to encourage each student to develop unique personal talents such as self-confidence. Without doubt this effort is more pronounced in the private sector with its smaller classes and elaborate facilities, but the outstanding public sector has similar goals and purposes.

In order to meet these diverse goals, while still remaining faithful to the overriding academic perspective, a broad and flexible curriculum is provided by our Western schools. Again this is more obvious at the private schools, where music and the arts play a very conspicuous role in the educational facilities and activities. Extracurricular activities are given much emphasis with sports facilities at most of our private schools, rival-ing those of many nearby institutions of higher learning accommodating a similar number of students. In spite of the vigorous academic demands, it is a well-rounded education these future leaders of America and Britain are receiving, many in an environment, particularly in private schools, that imprints an indelible influence on their lives. As one American student described it, "I always get a lump in my throat when I spot the top of the central tower on campus coming back to school after vacations."

This type of reaction would be most unusual to our outstanding Japanese students simply because the atmosphere in their schools is so vastly different. One Japanese student got to the very heart of the matter when he said that his school was meant to prepare him to take the entrance examination, and that was all he expected of it. He would not expect to have the close supervision and individual monitoring that the private sector in the Western schools under review provide their students. In one of the private boarding schools in Britain a student explained that academically he was supervised by his academic advisor along with six other students, as well as his house master in the evenings, in addition to the regular classroom teacher in each subject.

With fifty or so students in the private classrooms of the outstanding Japanese schools, the teachers cannot, nor do they recognize the need to, monitor the individual development of their students except on the many mock tests administered by the school. Employing elaborate computer programs, the schools can carefully plot the progress of each student on the tests as the year progresses, providing the anxious parent a fairly accurate prediction of the child's chances of passing any one particular university entrance examination. From this perspective, there is little difference in the teacher's responsibility in Japan's outstanding public and private secondary schools since they both follow a similar approach to the education of the nation's future leaders.

Finally, the role of the school in inspiring leadership qualities among these outstanding students is of critical importance since their graduates will assume more than their share of positions of influence and power in later years. Once again, a major difference between Japan and the two Western countries becomes evident. There is an unstipulated practice among the outstanding schools of Japan not to actively promote leadership qualities among their highly select student body. Moreover, rather than appearing as a negative feature of these schools to the students and their parents, many of whom themselves have attained positions of influence, it is a virtue. In a word, the school is not expected to promote education specifically for leadership.

This approach toward leadership contrasts sharply with that followed by the outstanding schools of America and Britain. Although there is seldom a carefully defined written policy to develop and nurture leadership traits among their students, the opportunities to do so are inherent in the school structure itself. Indeed, one of the most attractive features of many of the most distinguished schools both in America and in Britain to parents who have attained leadership positions themselves are the many opportunities provided by the school to develop leadership among its carefully selected student body. These schools make every effort both to encourage leadership tendencies within the student and to instill aspirations to lead among those not so inclined when they enter the school. In the private sector the students are also often surrounded by reminders of past glories of the school including conspicuous portraits or inscribed names of distinguished statesmen, scholars, and in some instances prime ministers and presidents, who graduated from their schools to become truly outstanding leaders. It is all part of the school's efforts to prepare the future leaders to lead.

During a visit to one of our American private schools, the current edition of the very slick student newspaper provided a case in point. The lead article featured an upcoming address in a lecture series by a well-known U.S. senator. He was, to be sure, a graduate of that school not so many years ago. In an adjoining article, a review of a speech given in a different forum the previous week at the school by a distinguished psychologist from Yale University was described as enlightening. The title of his speech: Creativity. He had been invited by the mathematics department currently emphasizing problem solving in their curriculum. None of this would take place at our Japanese schools. It would be a rare event to have an academic speak to a high school student body on a topic such as creativity.

The contrasting approach to leadership in Japanese schools reflects the cultural mores and traditions of Japanese society itself, considered in more detail in later chapters. To stand out among your peers, for example, as a leader, invites widespread criticism. Modesty is a trait most admired within the society. A successful leader in Japan is often one who exhibits a degree of reticence, especially about personal leadership capabilities. A successful leader is often the one who does not appear to be a leader but, in fact, has gained power and influence through quiet negotiations behind the scenes.

Another attribute of a Japanese leader is the ability to work cooperatively within a group to promote a sentiment of unity and, of singular importance, harmony. The potential leader must sharpen the skills of quiet negotiation by being able to appear as a cooperative team member in the harmonious adjustment of various opinions. Ultimately the leader's opinion may prevail in the final decision. In other words, although the leader's influence was the dominant factor, the supporters must not feel that their opinions were ignored in the final decision-making process. It is a subtle art of leadership that prevails in Japanese society, not dependent upon sharp intellect, clever speaking and debating skills, or wit, characteristics admired among Western leaders.

It is precisely the intangibles involved in developing leadership qualities among the Japanese that cannot be readily incorporated into the school's program. It is, in fact, the lack of it that appeals to the students and many of their parents, simply because it cannot be taught. It is, as it were, subconsciously learned that most successful Japanese leaders do not stand out conspicuously. Consequently Japanese leaders rarely exhibit leadership traits associated with that concept as normally understood in the West. For example, many of the prominent American and British leaders have come through outstanding schools that cultivated debate through which students honed their skills of discourse and persuasion. That simply is not the case in the outstanding schools of Japan, where debate is virtually unknown and where simple discussion or give-and-take between teacher and student, or among students, in the classroom is not that common.

In a discussion among Japanese business leaders attending this researcher's weekly seminar for businessmen, a simple poll was taken of their perception of the incumbent prime minister. Their responses revealed the Japanese attitude toward leadership. Asked to evaluate the prime minister on a scale of 1 to 10, 1 being a very good prime minister and 10 a very poor prime minister, the average score was 2.5. These contemporary leaders of Japan gave him, as prime minister, a comparatively strong endorsement. They were then asked to evaluate the same individual not as prime minister but as a leader. The average score dropped precipitously to 8. To the same Japanese, their good prime minister was not a good leader.

Our Japanese business leaders clearly distinguished between a leader who stands out by taking decisive action in the Western sense and a leader who leads in the Japanese perspective by working within a group consensus striving for harmony. Their prime minister was not of the former. Even if he were, he could not lead in such a manner since his faction within the ruling political party was weak. He was dependent upon other factions for sustaining his position as a compromise candidate. Nevertheless he had gradually strengthened his influence within the party by quiet persuasiveness and sincere dedication to the job. A gradual improvement in the polls demonstrated that his style of leadership was being appreciated by the public. It would not likely be considered good leadership in the West.

As one member of the seminar, himself a very high ranking officer of Japan's most powerful business organization, described it, "Japan doesn't need strong political leaders." He was, indirectly, approving of his prime minister, who did not provide strong political leadership yet was judged a good prime minister. Without a strong political base, little if any charisma, no convincing political agenda, and no prior experience as a major political figure, the incumbent was serving rather effectively as Japan's prime minister even though few would call him an effective leader. Although he stood out at international meetings from his Western counterparts because he did not look or act like an international leader, at home his ratings as prime minister steadily improved.

Before moving on from the Japanese school and its effort, or the lack of it, to develop leadership qualities, the vital role of sports deserves our consideration. Paradoxically, in a school that is so inextricably involved in examination preparation, the premier event of the year is often the annual sports day or sports festival. Preparation for this special occasion becomes so consuming that it takes precedence over all other activities, including course work. Whether teachers and administrators approve of it or not, and there are those who do not, the sports festival carries a momentum of its own with which the school cannot interfere even if it wishes to curtail the excesses, including some of the very rough and dangerous physical events that challenge the students at several of our schools.

To a good many students, sports day represents the very heart or spirit of the school itself. When one student was asked if he would want his own child to attend his old school someday, only if the school maintains sports day as it is, was his surprising response. The concern was that the school administrators might attempt to curtail the event since it was all-consuming. He sincerely felt that the school spirit would be irrevocably destroyed without that great day. In fact, in this particular school from our select category, a very large number of senior students devote so much time to the sports festival they sacrifice university entrance for one year, entering a special commercial preparatory course to make up for the lost time devoted to the sports festival.

The significance of sports day in Japan's outstanding high schools has perhaps less to do with sports per se than with non sports-related factors. First of all, the general practice is that students assume primary if not complete responsibility for planning and conducting the entire event. This places an extremely heavy burden on the student committee and its leaders for the school's major event of the year when many spectators, both parents and graduates, attend. With the entire student body divided often into four groups for the various events, the opportunity for honing a sharp sense of competition is seized upon by the students with a vengeance. The amount of clamorous cheering that surrounds every event throughout the long day is followed, appropriately, by a school holiday for recovery. The school then returns to its normal academic pace until, long before the following year's sports festival, students begin to organize their teams for that one great spectacle of the year.

There are, consequently, some opportunities in our Japanese schools to develop leadership qualities among a limited number of students. As we have seen, they relate primarily to sports. The enormous enthusiasm that engulfs the student body for this annual event derives from the enthusiasm generated by the students themselves under student leadership chosen by themselves. It is through these opportunities that some of our future Japanese leaders come to experience firsthand how effective a team can be when united in its goals, and how individually gratifying it can be when your team competes effectively. The thrill of competition knows no bounds during the sports festival in the outstanding schools of Japan.

It is not coincidental that so many of the leaders of America and Britain, as in Japan, have also come from outstanding schools in the private sector. For it is especially among the private schools where the opportunities to develop leadership qualities abound. But the similarities between East and West end at that point. In our Western schools leadership training comes through an elaborate process of assigning various responsibilities for other students at various levels. It is most conspicuous at boarding schools in which student prefects or monitors are given leadership positions within their dormitory or house in some form requiring them to lead other students. This usually entails certain powers of discipline to enforce their decisions. It is the experience of serving as a leader of others that develops the leadership skills in our Western students under study, many of whom come from families where the father, and not infrequently the mother as well, are individuals of considerable influence within their fields of endeavor.

A senior student prefect at one of the British boarding schools involved in this project described his responsibility for taking roll and maintaining a reasonable degree of classroom discipline among the first-year students each morning, prior to the appearance of the teacher, as a very minor role. When asked how he accomplished this feat with a group of lively boys, he explained that he chose several of the more mature students to assist him. What this student leader was undergoing was not only the act of demonstrating leadership qualities himself; he was also passing that on to certain first-year students by assigning them responsibilities to lead others. Day in, day out, many of the future leaders of America and Britain are actively participating in the carefully designed and somewhat complex process of preparing to become future leaders by holding leadership roles within the school itself.

Assigning responsibility to students in the Western private schools in order to provide training experiences in leadership is not undertaken willy-nilly by the administrators and teachers. It is carefully planned and implemented by a most cautious process of selecting those worthy of the power these student positions command, and the benefits they derive, both physically and psychologically. But it goes beyond that. One headmaster spoke for many when he frankly explained that his very famous school could not operate for one week without the student prefects or monitors, such was the extent of their role in maintaining both student discipline and student morale. This was particularly true in the dormitory management as well as with the team sports and other social events of the school. Far from being contrived, student leadership was absolutely essential. One of the student prefects reinforced that conclusion accordingly: "I don't know how our school could manage without us." Apparently it could not.

As with the Japanese schools, sports play a similarly unique role in the Western schools as an integral part of leadership training. Sports represent the one common factor, other than university preparation, among our understanding Japanese and Western schols. Ironically, in schools that place such impressive numbers of their graduates in first-rate universities, sports would also be given such a prominent role in the daily life of the students. And in both the Eastern and Western private schools, in particular, students are given heavy responsibility in managing the sporting activities.

There are major differences, though. The Western private schools often devote blocks of periods nearly every day for sports. In one of the most famous British schools, the clicking of spikes on pavement most afternoons at two begins the parade of boys from their houses to the extensive playing fields for an afternoon of games. The competitive spirits rise to the occasion when one student house is pitted against another. The Japanese students, in contrast, will be practicing incessantly for the one big day of events. In both cases, students will be given, or in the case of the Japanese, will take, responsibility for managing most of it under student leadership. The other major difference is that the opportunities for leadership experience go well beyond sports only in the Western schools.

Witnessing the overt process of instilling leadership qualities in the future leaders of America and Britain, and the covert process the future leaders of Japan must acquire either intuitively or through extremely discriminitive ways, raises a highly significant question. How will the leaders of these three countries react to each other in the twenty-first century in the fields of government, business, education, and the various other sectors where leaders from their respective countries must negotiate with each other? We can only speculate, but the results of this survey presented in the following chapters should provide us with appropriate data to draw some convincing conclusions.

The major differences, then, among the outstanding schools that are educating the future leaders of America, Britain, and Japan are not between the public and private school education they are now receiving. Rather, our three nations can be loosely divided into two groups: the British and Americans on the one side, and the Japanese on the other; that is, the East and the West. Although there are certainly distinctions between the outstanding public and private school sectors in both America and Britain, collectively they are more similar to each other than to the Japanese. Other than the overriding motivation for university preparation to enter the best universities all three groups harbor, there is not too much the future leaders of Japan share in common with the future leaders of America and Britain in the education they are receiving in the outstanding schools of their respective countries. It is within this overall context that we now turn to a comparison of the attitudes and perceptions our outstanding students have of themselves, their future, their country and its future, and of each other.

NOTES

1. See D. Nimmo, ed., *Political Attitudes and Public Opinion* (New York: David McKay, 1972), p. 161; Sidney Kraus, *The Effects of Mass Communication on Political Behavior* (University Park: Pennsylvania State University Press, 1976), p. 17; Stanley Renshon, *Handbook of Political Socialization* (New York; The Free Press, 1977), p. 196; and Kent Jennings, *The Political Character of Adolescents* (Princeton: Princeton University Press, 1974), 252.

2. Thomas Dye, *Who's Running America?* (Englewood Cliffs, N.J.: Prentice-Hall, 1986), p. 1.

3. Ibid., p. 192.

4. *Fortune*, "Where the CEOs Went to College," June 18, 1990, p. 82.

5. William Domhoff, *Who Rules America Now? A View of the '80's* (Englewood Cliffs, N.J.: Prentice-Hall, 1983), p. 25.

6. Irene Fox, *Private Scholars and Public Issues* (London: Macmillan, 1985), p. 3.

7. A. Gidders, "The Anatomy of the British Ruling Class," *New Society*, Vol. 50 (1979): pp. 8-10.

8. *Diamond Shukan*, June 16, 1990, pp. 114-20.

9. Seikai Kancho Jinjiroku, Toyo Keizai, Tokyo, 1990.

2

SELF-IMPRESSIONS
OF FUTURE LEADERS

Leaders or Followers?

Most students enrolled in these outstanding schools in America, Britain, and Japan are well aware of their potentially privileged career opportunities. For those in the private sector in particular, this is one of the basic motives underlying the immense effort and expense they and their parents have devoted to get into these schools in the first place. But as teenagers, do they perceive themselves as leaders or future leaders? How important is it to them to enter the leadership ranks of their country? These questions were posed to all 3,000-plus students to ascertain the impression of themselves as it relates to their leadership roles in the twenty-first century (see Questions 1, 2, 3).

There appear to be significant, and understandable, differences between the attitudes of the future leaders of Japan and those of both America and Britain on the issue of leadership itself. This finding, in fact, may turn out to be one of the most important results of the study and an appropriate topic with which to initiate our analysis of the survey data. Although introduced in the opening chapter, the divergent interpretations of, and attitudes toward, leadership, central to this study, need further clarification in light of the above statistics.

The Western concept of leadership implies one who stands out from the others by exhibiting certain unique qualities that attract others to follow. We describe those who are very adept at this process as charismatic. The distinguished wartime leaders from the United States and Britain, Prime Minister Churchill and President Roosevelt, were prime examples of Western leaders endowed with charisma who were educated in outstand-

Question 1
How would you characterize yourself?

	Americans	British	Japanese
As a leader	51.0	36.1%	16.9%
As a follower	6.3	6.4	26.3
Neither	40.7	56.7	55.4

Question 2
Are you receiving an education that would enable you to become a leader in your field?

	Americans	British	Japanese
Yes	77.4%	65.1%	17.8%
No	6.3	11.3	32.5
No opinion	15.3	22.2	48.3

Question 3
How important is it to you personally to become a leader in your field?

	Americans	British	Japanese
Essential	23.2%	14.0%	23.0%
Very important	43.2	33.9	32.7
Somewhat important	27.0	38.0	26.8
Not important	5.5	13.1	16.8

ing schools similar to those in this study. Innumerable other figures from both countries fit into this category.

Few Japanese of the past or present can be described in Western terms as charismatic leaders who stand out by demonstrating unique qualities that attract others to follow. It is simply not part of the cultural tradition of the society. That obviously does not mean that Japan is a nation without leaders. Rather, it indicates that the Japanese have a divergent understanding of the concept of leadership befitting their leaders from that in the West.

Although the old and oft-quoted adage that describes a fundamental trait of Japanese society, the nail that stands out gets knocked down, has a negative implication, it continues to influence this generation of future leaders. The results of this study show that these outstanding Japanese students tend to be much more modest than their Western counterparts when it comes to extolling their own personal leadership qualities. They are all cognizant of the fact that they are studying in outstanding schools that produce more than their share of graduates who eventually gain positions of influence, that is, of leadership, in one field or the other. Nevertheless over three-fourths of our outstanding Japanese students are most reluctant to recognize themselves as leaders, implying they stand out among the others. It is, therefore, not surprising that far more American (51%) and British (36.1%) students perceive themselves as leaders in comparison to the Japanese (16.9%). Likewise, over one-fourth of the Japanese students modestly evaluate themselves as followers, that is, not standing out, compared to only 6% of the Western students.

These results reflect yet another difference in the cultural patterns between East and West. British and American students to a far greater degree than in Japan, as we have noted, are encouraged in the classroom to speak up, volunteer answers, and express personal opinions, in effect, standing out. One American student described it distinctly: "Your ideas are constantly being tested." The Japanese classroom atmosphere, including that in the most outstanding schools in the land, discourages student participation in part because of the great reluctance of the students to express themselves in a formal setting in front of their peers. Their fear of embarrassment, of the protruding nail getting knocked down, inhibits classroom participation and spontaneity.

Japanese society, broadly interpreted, tends to be critical of conspicuous individualism, which restricts the individual from actively being identified as one seeking to lead. Teenage students, including the outstanding respondents in this study, exhibit a naivete that renders them ill at ease and ambivalent about being considered future leaders. To stand out from the others makes them feel uncomfortable. Consequently only one in six Japanese students would be so bold as to characterize themselves as leaders, whereas one in two Americans and more than one in three British students declare themselves as leaders.

Contemporary Japanese society also discourages overt elitism, which suppresses many of those potential leaders from demonstrating their leadership capabilities. There has been a major effort, not orchestrated from above, however, to promote in the schools the concept of equality as the fundamental principle of the new postwar democratic society. That attitude introduces a certain element of unease among some of our students who recognize the inconsistency of their privileged status as students of these elite schools within the framework of postwar social equality. This egalitarian principle of Western-style democracy, in fact, reinforces the social custom not to stand out among others. Indeed there are perceptive Japanese who argue that Japanese society has been traditionally egalitarian, that the introduction of democracy by the Americans during the occupation period after the war merely codified already existing customs. One of our Japanese students reflected this feeling when he claimed that he and many of his classmates disliked any hint by school authorities that they were destined for leadership, although all were aware of it.

The rather high percentage of students from all three countries who describe themselves as neither leaders nor followers brought a similar explanation from most of the students interviewed from the American and British schools, in contrast to the interviews with the Japanese students. The Western students made it clear that they did not, to be sure, consider themselves followers. However, the indisputable fact that so many of their classmates were potentially strong leaders made it difficult for those less endowed to perceive themselves as leaders. The internal competition for leadership in these schools is severe and the standards demanding. Under ordinary circumstances in regular schools, many of our Western students who chose the middle road in this survey would consider themselves as leaders.

The Japanese explained why one out of four fellow students describe themselves as followers, compared to only 6% of their Western peers who place themselves in that position. To these students enrolled in the best schools in the land, only the top students among them will attain the leading positions in society, which they envision as, for example, presidents of major companies. In other words, they set a very high standard for their category of leaders, understandable among such a group of students in such prominent schools. They also felt that the 55% who claimed they were neither leaders nor followers found the middle ground most comfortable for them, following Japanese custom. They sincerely believe they are neither and would probably feel the same way even if enrolled in ordinary schools.

The sense of modesty on the part of Japanese youth predictably carries over into the evaluation of their own school. This is in spite of the fact that the Japanese students are as cognizant of their school's record in placing an inordinately large number of graduates in the most prestigious universities in the land as are the Western students studying in their outstanding high schools. If that were not the case, most of them would not have made such an enormous effort to get into these schools.

The extremely high percentage of American (77.4%) and British (65.1%) students who believe their schools are preparing them to become leaders (Question 2), compared to 17.8% of the Japanese, reflects the atmosphere within the schools themselves. As noted, many of our Western schools in this survey have as one of their basic purposes the development of leadership traits that sets them apart from the average school. On the other hand, the outstanding Japanese schools, both public and private, make little conspicuous effort to encourage leadership, except in sports events, with characteristics similar to ordinary schools. In addition, there is a higher level of tension in all our Japanese schools attributable to the critical importance of examination preparation, in comparison to the noticeably more relaxed and consequently more enjoyable atmosphere in outstanding American and British schools. It is, therefore, more readily understood why the Japanese students have a less favorable attitude toward their school as it relates to developing leadership qualities than the students in the American and British schools. There simply is little overt effort on the part of the Japanese schools to impart a sense of leadership among the students, contrary to the Western schools.

Finally, the teachers and administrators of the outstanding schools of Japan do not generally possess a sense of obligation for the development of leadership among their students. Their primary task is to make every effort to see that their students are adequately prepared to take, and pass, the entrance examinations to the most famous universities. Leadership, character building, personality development—traits that a good many of the outstanding schools in America and Britain consider fundamental to their program and are not reluctant to boast about—are of minor concern to those responsible for the outstanding schools in Japan.

It would be misleading and inappropriate to give the impression that these Japanese schools are devoid of any concern for student standards other than academic. On the contrary these schools all set a very high moral standard of honesty, punctuality, personal integrity on examinations, respect for other students and the teachers, along with a great effort to discourage smoking and drinking and encourage a proper code of conduct both in and out of school. Above all, the outstanding schools of Japan assume as one of their primary responsibilities the encouragement of all students to exert maximum effort, at personal sacrifice if necessary, to accomplish their goals whatever they may be. At the moment they are, of course, overwhelmingly academic. However, the honing of a personal desire to do one's best, to always seek to perfect oneself, is the indelible stamp these outstanding Japanese schools imprint on the future leaders of the nation. But again, these goals are not that different from those in the regular schools of Japan since this attitude permeates Japanese society.

The responses to the third of the three questions concerning leadership are the most revealing. And it is here that a convergence of attitudes is readily detected. In this question there is no assessment of the individual student's personal qualities, which the Japanese would mitigate, but of one's goal in life. Among the four possible responses to the question of the personal importance of actually becoming a leader, the first two choices, "essential" and "very important," were purposely designed as extraordinarily strong attitudes. When you combine the responses of these two categories, a convergence appears more prevalent, with 66.4% of the Americans, 55.7% of the Japanese, and 47.9% of the British students revealing a sense of determination to become future leaders. There is a strong commonality in the personal goals of these outstanding students in all three countries. Many of them know where they are going, and it is crucially important for them to attain that goal. As one American student describes it, "We are all goal-oriented."

Once again the Japanese responded with considerably more restraint in Question 4 than their Western peers. Although undoubtedly cognizant that they sit at the pinnacle of the educational ladder at the secondary school level, the conditions under which they experience daily life, both at home and school and in between, cannot be described as very pleasant or accommodating. The academic pressure is severe, the classrooms crowded, the family expectations very high, the homes and apartments oftentimes small and crowded, the commuting trains suffocating, and leisure facilities available at a grossly distorted premium. In addition many of the students attending these outstanding schools will also enroll in classes at commercially run cram schools during holiday periods to go beyond the classroom requirements, always seeking a better chance to pass the examination at the very best universities. In light of these difficult conditions, it could be considered remarkable that only about 50% of the Japanese students are dissatisfied with the way things are going in their lives, in spite of their privileged status as select students studying in the most outstanding schools in Japan, well along on the road to success.

The low rates of dissatisfaction among American and British students, in contrast, are equally understandable. To be bright and energetic, as these students have proven to be, experiencing the challenges their schools provide along with the demands, the opportunities, and the comforts surrounding them, should result in a high level of satisfaction. Since they also have much attention placed on their individual development, certainly more so in the private sector but still an important concern in these outstanding public schools as well, there is a sense of communal effort that can be satisfying. It is simply not so in the outstanding schools in Japan. The differing responses of the students bear this out.

Question 4
In general, are you satisfied with the way things are going in your life today?

	Americans	British	Japanese
Very well satisfied	27.4%	17.8%	5.3%
Satisfied	56.9	63.8	45.1
Dissatisfied	12.5	14.9	37.7
Very dissatisfied	1.9	2.8	10.6

The ultimate purpose of most of our students in all three countries focuses on the preparation for university entrance. They have devoted much of their youthful energies not only to enter these outstanding secondary schools, but they have for the most part also concentrated much of their daily life after entry in keeping up with the educational demands placed upon them. A comparison of the attitudes toward the academic requirements of the school is an important consideration of this study (see Questions 5, 6, 7).

Question 5
How concerned are you about preparing for the examinations for university entry?

	Americans	British	Japanese
Deeply concerned	30.2%	52.0%	44.8%
Somewhat concerned	45.6	39.0	40.1
Not very concerned	16.3	5.3	11.8
Unconcerned	6.9	3.2	2.3

Question 6
How much time during an average weekday evening do you devote to academic study?

	Americans	British	Japanese
Under an hour	9.0%	9.8%	12.6%
1 to 2 hours	26.0	42.3	27.0
2 to 3 hours	37.1	36.1	43.3
4 or more hours	26.6	11.5	16.3

Question 7
How important is it to you personally to receive good grades?

	Americans	British	Japanese
Essential	19.4%	32.0%	12.4%
Very important	53.5	46.8	30.8
Somewhat important	24.2	18.7	40.5
Not important	2.5	2.1	16.0

These statistics reveal a consistency on the first two questions (5, 6). The pervasive goal of virtually all of the schools included in this survey is, as we have seen, to place as many of their graduates as possible in the finest universities available. The overriding concern of their students in this effort is to be expected. Although the role of the university entrance examination in Japanese education is notorious, entering a prominent university is the most powerful motive common to the outstanding students and their schools in all three countries. The time spent on daily homework is indicative of this.

The reaction to school grades (Question 7) is a reflection of their use in determining university entry. Good secondary school grades are much more important to the American student since most university admissions procedures consider them in the final decision. They are not the deciding factor, but to certain American university admissions officers, high school grades are one of the important elements in the fateful decision to admit, or not to admit. They are less important to the British student except for those applying for early approval under the special admissions process to such universities as Oxford and Cambridge that attract the very top students, in which secondary school performance is given serious consideration even before the so-called A-level entrance examinations are administered.

On the contrary, Japanese university entrance procedures ordinarily give no consideration to high school grades, except in the case of the very limited number of students accepted to certain private universities upon the recommendation of the secondary school principal. In the case of this writer's private university in Tokyo, the admissions procedure deliberately ignores high school grades, placing virtually total weight on the university entrance examination results calculated through a computer program. Again, this does not apply to the 10% or so of the high school recommendees who are not required to sit for the examination. Therefore it is imperative for most Japanese students to score the highest possible score on the entrance examination, not on their secondary school tests that determine their internal grades. Even though there is a natural relationship, the distinction between the two is clear to both Japanese students and their teachers.

There are two results that stand out among the responses to Question 8. First of all, the largest number of students among the future leadership classes of these three countries planning as their long-term career goals to enter the natural science field is found among the Japanese. The lowest percentage is seen with the British students. The differences, although not extreme, are still a barometer of the role of science in the respective school systems in which the Japanese give such an important role to science education from the very first grade onwards. It is, in fact, at the elementary school level where the basic knowledge and attitudes toward science

Question 8
Which subject area do you plan to study at the university?

	Americans	British	Japanese
Humanities	32.8%	26.6%	35.5%
Natural sciences	22.2	18.9	28.5
Business	20.6	24.2	20.9
Other	21.6	28.6	13.3

are developed, and it is at this level that the Japanese school system is so effective.

These results may portend further technical advances of Japanese industry for the twenty-first century in the enormously competitive field of high technology, in which the Japanese have demonstrated an advanced capability. Already the Japanese are producing about twice as many engineers annually as the Americans, and certainly many more in comparison to the British. On the other hand the number of students going into the rapidly expanding area of business is similar among the three countries, about one in four. It would appear that the balance between science and business among the Japanese may be more favorable for them to meet the demands and challenges of the twenty-first century of high technology than for their competitors, the Americans and British, among others.

One in ten Americans and one in fifteen British students chose foreign languages as the subject they like best, whereas one in four Japanese prefer the same subject (see Question 9). Negatively 21% of both American and British students like to study foreign languages the least compared with 12.9% of the Japanese. In fact, foreign language study is the subject receiving the lowest negative response by the Japanese. It ranks fairly high in the negative column for both the American and British students.

There are several ironies here. First of all, virtually all of the Japanese students study English in school four or five times per week as a near-compulsory course from the seventh to the twelfth grades, that is, from twelve to eighteen years old, for a total of six years. The emphasis is overwhelmingly on the written form with a concentration on translation exercises from English to Japanese, and the tedious memorization of grammatical rules necessary to pass the university entrance examination on English required by most institutions. Few students have an opportunity to speak the language during class. Consequently very few acquire an oral skill in this foreign language to use it in any practical way during their school days.

On the contrary, foreign languages are not usually introduced in

Question 9
Which subject among the following do you like the most?
The least? (in parentheses)

	Americans	British	Japanese
English	23.4%	21.2%	12.4%
(Japanese for the Japanese)	(13.9)	(11.1)	(18.4)
Foreign language	9.9	14.8	25.1
(English for the Japanese)	(21.4)	(21.3)	(12.9)
Mathematics	18.6	15.6	19.8
	(30.2)	(24.9)	(27.7)
Science	22.1	24.8	14.8
	(14.9)	(22.6)	(24.5)
History	23.8	22.6	27.0
	(15.5)	(18.4)	(13.7)

American schools at age twelve, nor required for six consecutive years. Indeed, many American universities require only one or two years of study of a foreign language as an entrance requirement. Some do not require a foreign language at all. Few require it as an integral part of an entrance examination. The results of this survey indicate that perhaps the American students are living in a society that does not place great emphasis on foreign languages, nor are they sufficiently involved in foreign language study in school to appreciate the subject. The British case is not that far removed from the American. In other words the degree of exposure to, and general attitudes toward, a foreign language may be a factor in the very low regard large numbers of our Western students give to the subject, although the schools in this study place more emphasis on foreign languages than do ordinary schools. Some of the British students felt that the special role Latin and Greek, treated as classical languages, have traditionally played especially in their private sector may put some of their students off languages.

There is another element affecting these results. English has become the international language of travel, business, science, diplomacy, sports, and a host of other areas as well. English-speaking students do not face the urgency of learning a foreign language when they can, so to speak, get by without it much more readily than the Japanese. Many of the future leaders of Japan realize their careers could be greatly enhanced if they acquire a basic knowledge of the international language of English. Consequently they take the study of this foreign language very seriously. English is, for example, one of the most popular courses for Japanese students to study in the after-school, weekend, and holiday courses at private institutions called *juku* found in all major cities. Although the

Japanese students were not polled on the issue, it can be assumed that a good many of our respondents enroll in English *juku* classes sometime during their secondary schooling.

These conditions, then, reflect the role foreign languages play in these three societies. For example, few British and American students take the initiative to enroll in private foreign language courses during their secondary school career, in contrast to the Japanese. All of their future leaders take at least four classes a week in foreign language study at school, plus supplementary classes for many of them before entering university. After entry, they will continue the study of English, many during their entire four years. What difference this makes to the future leaders of these three societies in the area of mutual understanding and international diplomacy is a matter of conjecture. Manifestly it gives the Japanese leaders in business and finance an edge over their Western counterparts in the intense competition to develop markets for products in the opposite countries.

A clear difference of opinion appears in student attitudes toward the teaching of their mother tongue. The course in the Japanese language ranks as the subject Japanese students like the least. On the other hand English is a fairly popular subject for both the American and British students. In their interviews Japanese students expressed the reaction that Japanese is one of the most difficult courses in the curriculum with extremely demanding requirements in the memorization and use of written symbols, based on the Chinese characters. Although many students find the course strenuous and oftentimes tedious, the result is the highest national literacy rate in the world.

American and British students do not view the course in English as particularly demanding and find a certain degree of enjoyment in the way it is taught in a more relaxed atmosphere. The Western students also are required to write many original essays in English on broad issues and topics, while the Japanese are seldom required to write original material of any complex nature. They are, in contrast, heavily involved in memorizing tedious Chinese ideographs and their use in preparation for the very demanding university entrance examination on the Japanese language included on every test.

The other curious result is that although a higher percentage of Japanese students (28.5%) than American (22.2%) and British (18.9%) plan to enter the natural science field, fewer Japanese (14.8%) like science as a course of study in secondary school than their American (22.1%) and British (24.8%) counterparts. This reflects the divergent approaches to science teaching. In the Japanese secondary school classroom, in sharp contrast to the elementary classroom, it is taught basically as a course in the memorization of great amounts of factual information requiring a tremendous amount of time and effort to keep pace with the demands for the notoriously difficult university entrance examinations on science. Students in the interviews complained passionately about the vast amounts of factual memorization required in the course of study that they found terribly boring.

According to the Western student interviews, this is in contrast to the more speculative approach in the American and British secondary classrooms of our outstanding schools, where considerable attention to enquiry is given in the science courses. In other words, it is a more interesting approach designed to encourage independent thinking and, to a certain degree, scientific innovation. It may be a factor in the comparatively high number of Nobel prizes awarded to American and British scientists, in comparison to the five or so Japanese scientists who have been selected for the prize in spite of the high standards of the subject in Japanese schools. Indeed, one of the Japanese winners spent much of his professional career at an American research institute where he claims his creative talents were more readily nurtured and appreciated.

Mathematics falls into a similar category. The Japanese are well-known for their success in international tests of mathematical achievement. Yet mathematics is liked the least among the subjects listed by the highest percentage of students (27.7%). According to the interviews, students claimed that the standard of mathematics in these outstanding schools is so extraordinarily high that it has become very demanding and extremely difficult for the students to keep pace with the course. This is, of course, a reflection of the academic standards of Japan's outstanding high schools. Even so, many of the students will enroll in private *juku* courses in mathematics in their unrelenting pursuit of successful performance on the university entrance examination. The very fact that only 50% of the entering students in Tokyo University come directly to the university from the high school is certain evidence that the other half have spent an entire full-time year in a *yobiko*, or "cram" school, undertaking intensive study of mathematics, Japanese, and English, among other subjects.

In regard to politics, a pattern across the three nations is evident (see Question 10). Few students in any country consider themselves far left or far right. This is not a generation of budding radicals destined for future leadership on either side of the political spectrum. Far from it. The largest grouping in all three countries falls within the category of either middle-of-the-road (America: 35.8% and Japan: 52.3%) or conservative (Britain: 41.2%). If the three categories starting from the center to the right including middle-of-the-road, conservative, and far right are combined, a large percentage of the future leaders of America (60.5%), Britain (78.1%), and Japan (73.4%) classify themselves as less than liberal in a political context. There seems little doubt that family background plays an influential role in their political persuasion since nearly all students interviewed classified their fathers as conservative. Against the back-

Question 10
How would you describe your political views?

	Americans	British	Japanese
Far left	3.6%	5.6%	2.7%
Liberal	33.9	15.0	21.5
Middle-of-the-road	35.8	30.9	52.3
Conservative	22.4	41.2	18.5
Far right	2.3	6.0	2.6

ground of long tenures of conservative central governments in all three countries, these results indicate that there may be more of the same moderate to conservative persuasion among the decision makers in the twenty-first century.

Among the three groups, however, the Americans express the most liberal attitudes, with one out of three casting themselves in this category. Student interviews, notably from the private sector, revealed that the liberal students were most active on campus, making the most noise as an expression of rebellion against their conservative parents. Some of the younger teachers in these schools encouraged such tendencies with progressive opinions integrated into their teachings. Japanese teachers at the outstanding schools are not known for encouraging liberal political thoughts in the classroom where examination preparation is the major concern.

The interviews also revealed a major difference between the Japanese and British students, in contrast to the Americans, for the basis of their political attitudes. Many British and Japanese students explained that their moderate political stance was not based on support of the conservative party in power for so many years in their respective countries. Rather, it derived more from their distrust of the opposition socialist parties that supported policies the students felt had little promise for improving their country based on socialist ideology. The American students do not interpret the differences between the Republican and Democratic parties in ideological terms, but find themselves simply more comfortable with moderate principles, in spite of the fact that some of them are passing through a stage of rebellion against their parents.

We turn now to a series of questions concerning topics that are either close to the daily lives of some of our respondents, and/or are major issues in the societies of one or all of the three countries. The responses reveal what type of individuals we are dealing with as they react to social concerns.

There is an overwhelming endorsement among the three nationalities, from 85% (British) to 87% (Americans) to 94% (Japanese), of the concept that drugs are dangerous (see Question 11). Just over one in ten American

Question 11
Do you believe that drugs are dangerous to your health?

	Americans	British	Japanese
Very dangerous	55.7%	52.1%	74.5%
Dangerous	32.0	32.2	19.6
Not too dangerous	9.7	10.2	4.1
Not dangerous	1.9	3.4	1.6

and British students, along with one in five Japanese students, believe the contrary. These are outstanding students who have worked diligently to enter their outstanding schools. And most realize, too, that personal involvement with drugs could subject them to suspension from school, thereby casting them from the course they worked so hard to enter and that will most likely lead to a successful career. Their attitude toward drugs reinforces the general conclusion, supported by the personal interviews, that these outstanding schools are not confronted with a serious drug problem. It also points to a deep concern over the effects of drugs when our students become leaders in the future. Even though the Japanese have been able to maintain a relatively drug-free society, in comparison to the widespread use of drugs in America and the less frequent use in Britain, all three groups of outstanding students take a very negative attitude toward drugs.

The pattern among the 3,000 students in our three countries with respect to religion is clear (see Questions 12, 13). With one minor deviation, as the category becomes more negative toward religion, the number of students increases. The presence of religion in one's life as not important, and the expression of little confidence in organized religion, attracts the largest percentage in each group. The fact that 77% of the Japanese students feel religion is not important to them, and 83% show little confidence in any religion, is readily understood considering the role of religion in contemporary Japanese society. Only a relatively small number of the population would consider themselves religiously committed.

The Japanese public school system has also been totally secularized since the war. Some would argue that it was secular before the war as well. There are private religious schools in Japan, and one, a Christian secondary school, is included in our survey, but few of their students would classify themselves as Christians. The vast majority of Japanese students, although they know how to perform simple religious routines followed through the centuries, lack personal religious convictions. To many, religious bodies represent money-making organizations seeking political influence, which do not possess the solutions to social problems facing these students.

Question 12
How important to you personally is religion in your life?

	Americans	British	Japanese
Essential	17.6%	12.3%	3.7%
Very important	15.9	13.0	4.0
Somewhat important	28.9	27.5	14.8
Not important	36.7	47.0	77.0

Question 13
How much confidence do you have in organized religion?

	Americans	British	Japanese
Much	21.3%	11.7%	2.1%
Some	34.6	34.6	14.4
Little	43.0	52.9	83.0

What is most revealing is the degree to which contemporary students in the outstanding schools in America (36.7%) and Britain (47%) do not perceive religion as important in their lives. Moreover, 43% of Americans and 52.9% of the British show little confidence in organized Christian religion. It is worth noting that in both of these Western countries schools evolved from the Christian church. Most denominations once viewed these schools with unsurpassed zeal as instruments of the church to maintain, strengthen, and spread religious convictions. And well after the public schools in both Britain and America became in essence secular or near-secular, many private schools in each country exemplified their religious heritage by required chapel and other forms of Christian ceremonies.

Even to this day, the traditional relationship between the Christian religion and many of the private schools included in this survey is evident with a chapel situated prominently at the center of the campus, although of diminishing importance. An American student expressed a rather common feeling that his private school with its central chapel was purposely moving away from any religious relationship. Even so, required chapel is still conducted at a few institutions among the British Public Schools in our study. But only about one student in three attaches much importance to religion in their lives in spite of the fact that about half of our American respondents, and well over half of the British, attend private schools with a Christian foundation. Both groups also originate in societies that not too many years past could be characterized without much disagreement as Christian countries. The American public schools in this study are essentially secular while the British public sector has tenuous ties to certain religious bodies.

The failure to cultivate strong religious convictions among this generation of top students, many of whom attend schools with a religious background, is strong evidence of the secularization of prominent Western countries. It may also be an important factor during the twenty-first century when church and state relationships come under dispute, as they inevitably will in both Britain and America. A further separation can be anticipated when this generation of secondary school students enters the leadership class of the next century.

In an effort to determine how concerned these future leaders are for their own well-being, and the well-being of others, a series of related questions was posed to all of the students (see Question 14).

Question 14
How important to you personally are the following?

	Essential	Very important	Somewhat important	Not important
- Being well-off financially -				
Americans	24.3%	39.2%	31.4%	4.4%
British	20.9	38.1	34.7	6.1
Japanese	22.7	38.9	30.5	7.8
- Helping others who are experiencing difficulty -				
Americans	27.8%	48.1%	21.5%	2.3%
British	15.7	44.1	35.5	4.2
Japanese	24.8	39.1	30.6	5.2
- Being popular among my classmates -				
Americans	5.4%	24.6%	55.1%	14.3%
British	12.1	39.9	39.2	8.2
Japanese	7.1	21.4	44.4	26.4
- Having a good relationship with my family -				
Americans	52.2%	34.6%	11.1%	1.9%
British	54.2	31.5	11.4	2.8
Japanese	36.6	36.6	20.6	6.0

Close agreement appears on the question of being well-off financially, with approximately 60% of each of the three groups placing great significance on having money. It appears as a prime motive behind the enormous efforts these able students have made to get into their outstanding secondary schools in all three countries. Similarly there is a strong feeling of importance among a solid majority in each country to help others in difficulty. But clearly there is a far greater involvement of students in volunteer and charitable activities in the Western schools, more so in the private sector, than is found in the Japanese schools. Such activities are greatly restricted in a school designed for test preparation. Nevertheless our private Western schools are also deeply involved in academic preparation for university entrance exams; yet they have traditionally emphasized service in an effort to broaden the perspective of their students, many of whom come from families of considerable financial means.

Being popular among one's classmates is not essential to many students in each country. However, the Japanese appear less concerned with peer attitudes than their Western counterparts, in spite of their reticence to speak out in front of peers in class. Partial explanation for this relates to the personal intensity among the Japanese students in their single-minded devotion in preparing for the university entrance examinations. Moreover there is an implication in Japanese society that being popular signifies an attempt to stand out among your peers, referred to previously. If the phrase had been "liked by your classmates" rather than being popular, it is estimated that a much stronger importance by the Japanese would be given to the former concept, which does not imply individual popularity.

Family relationships remain a strongly held commitment in the lives of all three groups. A positive majority in each country believes that a good relationship with one's family is either essential or very important. Among these three, however, the Japanese curiously place less importance on the family. It has been suggested by one teacher involved in the project, and reinforced by student interviews, that this could be attributed to the lack of influence by the father. In the Japanese middle class, from which so many of our participants originate, fathers in the business world devote very long hours to their company, spending little time at home when their children are present. It is not uncommon for the father not to see his children from Monday to Saturday, or to have only fleeting encounters with them during the work week, arriving home after ten o'clock in the evenings. The basic assumption in the Japanese family is that the mother assumes primary responsiblity for the child's welfare, particularly in educational matters.

In order to more fully understand how our future leaders perceive themselves and their own people, each group was asked to make a self-evaluation according to certain traits (see Tables 7, 8, 9). Included among them are concepts closely associated with each of the three peoples.

Table 7
American student perception of the American people

	Not very				Highly
	1	2	3	4	5
Creative	1.4%	3.7%	17.7%	39.1%	31.8%
Loyal	3.7	11.8	34.3	27.4	16.9
Emotional	0.6	2.7	13.0	37.7	39.5
Materialistic	0.5	0.3	4.9	22.8	65.6
Individualistic	1.3	4.7	15.0	27.1	45.6
Industrious	1.8	8.2	30.1	35.7	16.9
Generous	3.9	13.1	37.4	26.8	12.6
Trustworthy	4.3	15.5	40.8	22.9	9.9
Polite	8.9	20.1	39.0	18.5	6.9
Forgiving	3.8	12.5	41.1	22.9	13.2
Aggressive	0.7	1.2	14.3	36.0	40.9
Intelligent	2.0	4.3	23.6	40.6	23.1

Beginning with the most extreme results in Table 7, only one trait draws more than half of all American respondents in the category highly of number 5. American youth consider themselves and their fellow countrymen, more than any other category, as highly materialistic (65.6%). Next in order are highly individualistic (45.6%) and highly aggressive (40.9%). On the other hand, the smallest percentage of Americans choosing this category of highly is associated with highly polite (6.9%), highly trustworthy (9.9%), and highly forgiving (13.2%). Highly loyal (16.9%) and highly industrious (16.9%) tied for fourth place from the bottom.

The differences between the top three traits, materialistic, individualistic, and aggressive, and four of the bottom five, polite, trustworthy, forgiving, and loyal, can be seen in the degree of hardheadedness or no-nonsense style, competitiveness, and go-getting traits our American students attribute to the American character. The top three portray the spirit of activity and boldness versus the quiet character of the more

Table 8
British student perception of the British people

	Not very				Highly
	1	2	3	4	5
Creative	2.3%	13.6%	34.3%	29.9%	18.7%
Loyal	3.1	8.7	28.1	34.4	24.4
Emotional	4.3	14.5	29.1	33.3	17.3
Materialistic	1.6	5.7	30.9	41.3	18.7
Individualistic	2.3	8.2	27.3	38.0	22.2
Industrious	5.2	18.9	42.0	25.7	6.8
Generous	3.6	12.5	30.5	34.9	17.3
Trustworthy	3.4	11.9	36.7	31.3	14.6
Polite	5.1	15.7	29.6	29.2	18.8
Forgiving	5.4	17.8	38.7	26.6	9.6
Aggressive	3.8	13.8	36.5	30.8	13.5
Intelligent	3.0	5.5	32.2	38.4	19.0

passive politeness and forgivingness at the bottom. The image of an American by these Americans is one of power, forthrightness, even crudeness, which all characterize the frontier spirit. Some would call it the John Wayne syndrome of the Old West, a uniquely American phenomenon apparently still pervading American youth.

These strong traits of Americans, as perceived by the future leaders of America, could exert an underlying influence on American leadership in the twenty-first century when these teenagers assume decision-making responsibility. Those who enter American politics must appeal to the perceived character traits of their constituency in order to get elected, and reelected. Those who enter business and the professions must exert that strong form of leadership they perceive as the American way of free enterprise. Those who develop foreign policy must demonstrate that America deals with the world from a position of strength. When these results are placed within the context of the famous description by former American

Table 9
Japanese student perception of the Japanese people

	Not very				Highly
	1	2	3	4	5
Creative	19.9%	29.8%	23.3%	15.9%	9.5%
Loyal	4.6	7.7	17.0	30.7	38.2
Emotional	8.5	23.2	36.9	16.9	12.4
Materialistic	1.7	5.3	15.8	31.9	42.9
Individualistic	12.4	21.6	26.6	19.7	17.6
Industrious	0.9	2.4	8.1	24.2	62.7
Generous	7.6	14.3	37.4	26.5	12.1
Trustworthy	8.0	15.9	37.9	23.9	11.9
Polite	5.0	9.3	26.7	32.5	24.5
Forgiving	8.2	20.6	36.9	21.3	11.1
Aggressive	16.2	38.0	31.9	7.9	4.1
Intelligent	5.1	7.1	27.6	36.8	21.6

ambassador to Japan, Mike Mansfield, that the most important bilateral relationship in the world is that between Japan and the United States, they have a highly significant meaning to the future leaders of Japan.

The curious result of only 16.9% choosing highly industrious, in describing the American character, could be of some concern to those long accustomed to a more idealistic image of American society. The traditional image of the American as portrayed in textbooks, films, novels, and folklore has been closely related to the concept of industriousness associated with hard work. Apparently one of the most cherished and admirable traits historically attributed to the American character is no longer considered an accurate portrayal by this generation of outstanding youth. The decline of American influence in global affairs, perhaps interrupted temporarily by the Gulf War, and the apparent decline in American industrial productivity, in comparison to other countries such as Japan, is a factor influencing this new image of American industriousness, according to students during the interviews. One student summed up a prevalent attitude among them succinctly: Once we were ahead, but we have slacked off and are falling behind others like the Japanese.

Other traits that received only a cautious and somewhat surprising response that contradicts the historical portrayal of Americans is highly generous (12.6%) and highly trustworthy (9.9%). America and individual Americans have been recognized throughout the world as extremely generous in the huge amounts of foreign aid extended, for example, with the massive Marshall Plan for devastated Europe after World War II. That generous act is commonly praised for laying the foundation for the economic revival of Western Europe and especially the economic miracle of America's major European wartime enemy, Germany. America's immense generosity likewise resurrected its Asian wartime enemy, Japan, building the base for its spectacular postwar economic miracle. Nevertheless, this generation of Americans is apparently unaware of the generosity of its people.

Even fewer American students (9.9%) felt that Americans are highly trustworthy. United States history has portrayed American society as effecting a resolute trustworthiness unequalled in world annals. Other peoples might be shifty, perfidious, and untrustworthy, but Americans as a democratic Christian nation could always be trusted to keep the faith and to preserve the democratic principles and the democratic way of life. This generation views the American character differently, with fewer than one in three choosing either of the two positive categories 4 and 5 for trustworthiness of Americans. The specter of crime and drugs in American communities influenced this negative reaction, according to the students in the interviews.

The future leaders of America demonstrate that they believe in only part of the traditional image of Americans that the schools themselves have taught each succeeding generation, accordingly: that Americans are individualistic, industrious, and trustworthy; and that in part due to these fundamental principles their unquestionable economic success has enabled Americans to be not only generous to those less fortunate, but materialistic in lifestyle as well. The materialistic and individualistic image has survived with this generation of outstanding students, but industriousness, generosity, and trustworthiness have not. It is far from an overall positive image of contemporary American society perceived by these future American leaders.

Conversely, Table 8 shows that not one trait attracted more than a fourth of the British students in their perception of their own people on category 5 (highly). Highly loyal received the largest number (24.4%) and highly individualistic the second highest (22.2%) on this strongest possible choice. In fact only one category, materialistic, attracted over 40% for any one number, 4 in this case. On the opposite extreme of not very (1), the highest percentage was 5.4% for not very forgiving. In general, then, the future leaders of Britain perceive themselves and their fellow countrymen in images that do not stand out dramatically. They contrast sharply with the Americans. Theirs is, rather, an image symbolic of a middle-of-the-roader, a plodder, the somewhat inconspicuous figure devoid of sharp-edged character.

However, in order to gain a better perspective, the two most positive columns of 4 and 5 must be added together. In that case 60% of the British students believe that their people are both materialistic and individualistic, representing the highest positive responses. Although not reaching the magnitude of the American student attitudes toward Americans, the same characteristics of materialistic and individualistic stood out in the highly category for both groups.

During the interviews with British students, one of the strongest images of their own people, and of themselves, was expressed frequently. The British people are seen by many of these students as individualistic, more so than the statistics indicate. And that individualism implies going their own way. "We are individualists" was expressed with a certain degree of pride and a touch of arrogance that other peoples were not, at least to the extent of the British. Another student reinforced the statistics from this study when she claimed that this generation of British youth is "the most materialistic ever."

The lowest percentage in column 5, only 6.8% for highly industrious, confirms the generally subdued and somewhat pessimistic perception of the British held by these young British students. Indeed, at the other extreme, one out of four chose the two negative categories (1 and 2) of not very industrious. Again during the many interviews with British students, this negative image was continually reinforced. The recurring theme centered on the word "downhill" to describe the current state of affairs in Britain.

As with the Americans, these reponses reveal how the present generation of British youth have edged away from an earlier perception of a highly endowed people leading the world into a new, industrialized civilization. In the earlier era the illustrious British exemplified the word "industry" itself, with its great entrepreneurial spirit of capitalism expanding the power and influence of a tiny island nation around the world. Nevertheless, to this generation, the British are no longer highly industrious. To many of our respondents, their nation is simply going downhill.

In Table 9, in marked contrast to both the American and British responses toward their own people, the major trait chosen by the Japanese students about themselves and their people is industriousness. For the Japanese participants, who have been very moderate throughout most of this survey, to have chosen the extreme category of highly industrious by a strong majority of 62.7% is impressive in itself. If the next most positive category of 4 is added to the response for 5, the total becomes an overwhelming majority of 86.9% of these 1,000 Japanese students who perceive their people in the strongest terms as industrious. The only other trait that stands out so vividly on any of the responses is materialistic on the part of the American students (65.6%) describing the American people.

An indication of the changing attitudes of our teenage participants is evident in the second most prominent category chosen by the Japanese. Surprisingly, 42.9% chose highly materialistic to accompany industriousness as the two strongest traits of the Japanese. Traditionally the Japanese have been known for a national ethic of frugality and saving. Recently, however, with economic success has come an enormous flood of available money unleashing an unprecedented spending spree, from expensive imported European luxury cars to condominiums in Hawaii. This generation of Japanese youth is the first to witness from childhood the fruits of an economic miracle surrounding them. It is surely the first to perceive their society with a new identity as materialistic, a concept traditionally associated with the West and epitomized by America.

On the opposite side, the Japanese have the strongest images among the three nationalities in the negative, or not very, rankings. To compare, the highest percentage among the British students about the British in the number 1 ranking is 5.4% for not very forgiving. With the Americans it is 8.9% for not very polite. The Japanese, however, registered a 19.9% for not very creative, 16.2% for not very aggressive, and 12.4% for not very individualistic in describing the Japanese people.

On the whole, then, our Japanese students perceive themselves and their people in more extreme forms than that of the comparable British results. From this perspective they are more similar to the Americans. However, the extreme forms are noticeable not only in the positive rankings of highly but also in the negative rankings of not very, led by the one-fourth who think of the Japanese as not very creative, a rather standard image of the Japanese also held by foreigners. When you add the second most negative ranking of 2 to number 1, nearly half (49.7%) of all the Japanese perceive themselves as not very creative.

This is a significant image of the Japanese by their future leaders as Japan takes an increasingly influential role in global affairs approaching the twenty-first century. It reflects a degree of modesty that permeates the social customs. But it also reflects a cultural pattern of inferiority displayed by the Japanese when dealing with Western peoples, particularly Caucasians. To many Japanese, for example, the Americans are truly creative while the Japanese are not; the Americans are individualists while the Japanese are not, and so on. The Japanese themselves eagerly await trends to develop in America in clothing style, music, consumer spending, and various social, commercial, and even political trends, among others, in order to predict the trends in Japan five years later, so the saying goes, with a good deal of validity.

The perceptions of the Japanese by their future leaders contrast sharply with both the perceptions of Americans by their youth and the perceptions of the British by their youth. They all obviously reflect cultural patterns under which the three groups have been brought up and to which they each are naturally accustomed. However, it is at the international stage where our future leaders will interact with each other in the many areas of contact as these outstanding students today, destined to represent their country in the twenty-first century, assume responsibilities for making policies that will affect us all. The next step in our study of the future leaders of America, Britain, and Japan, then, is to consider their attitudes toward their country and its institutions.

3

ATTITUDES TOWARD COUNTRY

Trust and Confidence

Many of our future leaders selected for this study are destined for important positions in various institutions of the society, including government service. Their influence on the formulation of national policy, both domestic and international, will undoubtedly be formidable. Thus their contemporary attitudes toward their country, its history, its government, and other national institutions are of critical importance to the future of their respective countries since the general attitudes they hold today as upper teenagers, we are informed by competent researchers, carry over into their adult lives.

The similarities of the answers to Question 15, with approximately 60% of all students agreeing with the statement, are somewhat surprising in view of modern history. Clearly the 56.9% of the Japanese students who are proud of their nation's history do not take pride in Japan's aggressive and brutal policies during World War II. Rather, the concept of Japanese history to them extends back to a much earlier period when the

Question 15
Our country has an historical tradition of which I am proud.

	Americans	British	Japanese
Agree	60.0%	62.3%	56.9%
Disagree	15.7	11.7	16.0
No opinion	22.4	25.4	24.6

nation of Japan was formed, around the sixth century, as the wise Prince Shotoku unified the country under his tutelage. During this long history the classical art traditions of Kabuki and Noh dances along with other dramatic forms, such as the Bunraku puppet, evolved. These are the elements of Japanese culture that come to the minds of our respondents when asked about their historical traditions. Although most of the students realize that these traditional aspects of early Japanese society are not well known or appreciated abroad, nor do they themselves know much about them, they still embody cultural forms of which many students are proud.

A more recent peak in prewar Japanese history occurred during the great Meiji Restoration of 1868 when, under enormous constraints, the feudalistic nation transformed itself into a fledgling industrialized nation building the foundation for its postwar status as an economic superpower. The Meiji era is studied in minute detail in Japanese history courses as every student learns about the dramatic events when Japan opened its society to the world, especially the West. Every generation of Japanese since that period learned how their country began the race to catch up to the industrialized Western powers then dominating the world. The generation currently in school is the first to be exposed to the many analyses, mostly from abroad, that that goal has finally been attained. Even though there are not a few among them, as we shall see with later questions, who still doubt that Japan has yet caught up with the West, the accomplishments of Japan in world history are a source of pride.

World War II, the great stain on Japanese history, is treated ever so lightly in school and in society in general. Our students do not have a guilt complex about a conflict that occurred many years ago and had no relation to them. There are those within Japan, including a few distinguished scholars, who argue that Japanese textbooks and history courses should expose the students to a more thorough analysis and description of events during that era, including objective teaching of the role of the emperor. There is, however, little attempt to do so. Therefore, to this youthful generation, witnessing only a nation emerging as a global economic power, World War II does not appear as an overwhelming blot in the entirety of a highly successful Japanese historical tradition extending from feudalism to super economic status in a little over a century. The majority of Japanese youth are obviously proud of their nation's historical performance.

The remaining 24% of the Japanese students who have no opinion about pride in their country's history reflect to some extent the experiences the postwar generation has encountered. In marked contrast to prewar and wartime Japan, when the ultranationalists gained control of the government inculcating the youth with the grossest concepts of

Japanese superiority, this generation seldom encounters nationalistic talk. For example, the Japanese public probably learns more about their postwar achievements from foreign reports than they do from sources within the country. They are subjected to a barrage of commentaries and statistics from the West, especially the United States, comparing their rates of growth and performance with those of other countries in a most favorable perspective.

The Japanese public, including the youth, find it very difficult to imagine that Japan is recognized abroad as an economic superpower, and that it is constantly being portrayed as a potential contender with America for global influence. It is not coincidental that one of the best-selling books in Japan during the 1980s, *Japan as Number One*, was written by an American. If a Japanese had written it, the book would have been dismissed by the Japanese as nonsense. Many felt the same way about the American book but found it fascinating simply because, even though the title's implication was incomprehensible to them, it was written by a distinguished American academic.

The national trait of modesty obviously includes perceptions about country. Except for the fringe elements running about the city streets on a weekend with loud martial music from the prewar era, the Japanese do not wave the flag of patriotism or promote the cause of nationalism in front of their youth. The flag itself is even an object of controversy as a result of World War II. It is rarely found in a Japanese classroom, a condition unimaginable to Americans for whom flag veneration has become part of the culture from the classroom to the church. Only recently has the Ministry of Education stipulated that the flag must be displayed during graduation exercises, an edict that has provoked a negative reaction among some sectors of the society.

American and British students are taught about their historical traditions with considerable confidence. The great British empire of the last century, extending from the tiny islands of the homeland around the world, is a monumental historical accomplishment of the British people that shines through the textbooks. Shakespeare, in a different context, dominates literature in much of the Western world, representing another great historical accomplishment of British culture, of which every student in this study is well aware. The majority of British students obviously take pride in those achievements.

American students receive a very strong dose of nationalism through their school's history courses in terms of the country's accomplishments, from the Declaration of Independence through the great victories of World War II. During election campaigns, politicians in general wave the flag of nationalism, periodically flooding the media with a powerful and oftentimes emotional sense of patriotism. The American public is continually reminded of the nation's everlasting respect for the founding fathers and their monumental contribution to modern democracy, the venerable United States Constitution.

Under these circumstances, then, it is rather surprising that 38% of American students and 37% of British students are either not proud of their country's historical tradition, or have no opinion about it. This deviates ever so slightly from the 40% of the Japanese who feel the same way about Japan's historical tradition. The interviews revealed that some British students are critical of their country's colonial policies of the past century that subjugated vast areas of the underdeveloped, and thereby defenseless, world to British authority. The legacy of race relations in the former colony of South Africa represents to some students a negative aspect of British history.

Some of the American students have not reconciled their country's involvement in Vietnam as an historical episode of which to be proud. They are periodically reminded of that most recent controversial war through highly popular films and television specials depicting American military power in unflattering images, inflicting cruel acts of punishment on the Vietnamese people. In addition, the era of slavery in the pre–Civil War American South stands out to some of our respondents as a permanent blight on the nation's history that balances out the successes.

During both the American and British student interviews, the influence of teacher attitudes was brought up. Most history teachers in these outstanding schools approach their nation's history in a fairly objective manner; that is, both sides of controversial issues and events are considered. Students consequently learn both the negative and positive factors that are often involved in well-known historical incidents. What may be taken by the general public as a glorious event in American history is shown to be not as positive and one-sided as commonly interpreted, which the students had not previously considered. The purpose is to instill into the future leaders a critical sense of reasoning toward not just their country's past but life in general. To some students it is confusing. To others it is the awakening or nurturing of a discriminating, some would call it cynical, attitude among this unique group of American students.

By contrast, Japanese history courses are taught primarily from a factual perspective for examination preparation, not to develop critical or discriminating thinking. For example, in one class attended by this researcher, the history teacher wrote on the board the names of a leading figure of the twelfth century who married a certain woman on a precise day in March in a precise year of the early 1100s. The students all copied it down in their notebooks since it just could possibly come up in an entrance exam at one of the universities. Our Western students do not study history in such a manner.

In addition, because Japanese history is long, dating into the ancient past, and taught with considerable detail, the time remaining for teaching about Japan's very recent history such as World War II is greatly curtailed. The still-controversial nature of the war is also a factor that induces some history teachers to avoid or gloss over that fateful episode in the nation's past. The students are aware of the general nature of the Pacific War and that Japan lost it primarily to the victorious American armies. The details, however, are avoided in class by many teachers, in comparison to the treatment of earlier Japanese history. The one-third of the students who expressed a negative or no opinion response concerning pride in Japan's history come out of this environment.

Although the percentage of American and British students who disagree with, or have no opinion about, pride in their national anthem may seem higher than anticipated (see Question 16), the negative reaction by the Japanese (50% disagree) is readily understandable. The unofficial Japanese national anthem, "Kimigayo," has become a controversial issue in postwar Japan. Until recently it was, in the minds of many young people, primarily associated with sumo wrestling since it was always played during the closing ceremony carried on nationwide television, or at Olympic events. It was seldom played at school ceremonies. To others its close relationship with and reference to the emperor has little meaning to them since the new emperor is remote from their lives, whereas the older generation had a much stronger relationship with long-reigning Emperor Hirohito.

The association between "Kimigayo" and national pride has not been emphasized in Japanese schools or society, in part because of its reference to the emperor, which was exploited by the militarist regimes before and during World War II for ultranationalist purposes. To counter the negative image of "Kimigayo" and to instill a greater sense of national pride among Japanese youth, the Ministry of Education ordered its rendition at major school events, including all graduation ceremonies beginning with the 1990 school year, in addition to displaying the flag. This controversial action provoked opposition by certain sectors of the society including, most noteworthy for our study, the powerful Japanese Teachers Union, Nikkyoso. Under these contentious conditions, it is understandable why

Question 16
I take pride in my country when I hear our national anthem.

	American	British	Japanese
Agree	59.4%	43.8%	21.7%
Disagree	16.3	30.1	49.9
No opinion	22.8	25.6	25.4

two-thirds of the Japanese students do not associate their unofficial anthem with national pride.

On the other hand, the fact that nearly 40% of these American youth and over 45% of the British do not have a feeling of national pride when they hear their national anthem may indicate a modern trend under way. Students from both countries felt that one of the major reasons for this reaction was the way the anthems are used. They have too often become associated with sporting events rather than pride in country. And when they are played for sporting occasions, the assembled spectators, especially in America, continue milling or walking about showing little respect for the anthem itself. It is difficult, therefore, for a substantial number from this generation to associate the tune with national pride. A traditional symbol of pride in nation, the national anthem does not apparently evoke the same patriotic spirit as it once did with previous generations. Other questions about attitudes toward country and government corroborate these results.

The future leaders of America, Britain, and Japan manifestly do not hold strong feelings of support for their current government and political leaders (see Questions 17, 18). Although only one in four British students, and about one in ten American students have much confidence in their government leaders, the miniscule one out of fifty Japanese students holding this attitude is highly significant. Indeed, only 2.2% consider Japanese political leaders trustworthy. Even the most positive group, the British, register only a 30% agreement that their political leaders are trustworthy. Among the three nationalities, Japanese youth are overwhelmingly negative toward their leaders in politics and government.

Question 17
How much confidence do you have in your government leaders?

	Americans	British	Japanese
Much	12.7%	26.3%	1.5%
Some	60.6	45.3	19.9
Little	26.7	27.6	77.0

Question 18
The political leaders of our country are trustworthy.

	Americans	British	Japanese
Agree	16.2%	30.0%	2.2%
Disagree	52.7	41.5	83.2
No opinion	29.7	28.1	12.7

Although there are no available statistics of a similar nature from an earlier period, one explanation for this very negative attitude by the youth of each nation toward their national leaders could conceivably be that the younger generation is traditionally critical of its older leaders, that this is not a new phenomenon. On the other hand, as indicated in previous questions, this is not a radical, or even very liberal, generation involved in our study of future leaders in three countries. In fact, they tend to lean a bit to the right rather than the left.

There is irony here. All three countries have been governed by conservative parties for a number of years. This generation of youth in these three countries has never experienced anything except conservative rule since they reached the age of puberty. This poll was conducted during the very conservative supremacy of Prime Minister Thatcher in England, and the transition from the staunchly conservative President Reagan well into the new era of a somewhat less ideologue, but nevertheless conservative President Bush. In Japan the survey covers the end of the era of the very conservative Prime Minister Takeshita into the equally conservative and short-lived tenure of Prime Minister Uno, both of whom left office under clouds of suspicion. These were followed by Prime Minister Kaifu, all from the same conservative party.

Distrust of political leaders in Western-style democracies is endemic. The press and TV media, the latter from which so many of our students claim to receive most of their knowledge about current events, are influenced to a considerable degree in each of our three countries by analysts critical of conservative governments. The youth in such open societies are exposed through the media to the human frailties of political leaders and their policies regardless of party persuasion. Exposure of political weaknesses, such as the Iran scandals during the Reagan administration singled out by American students, is considered by the media as a cherished responsibility. In other words this generation of youth in these three countries has experienced only protracted conservative leadership that has inevitably attracted widespread media and public antagonism over the years. Their critical perceptions are perhaps a natural development since politics can produce unseemly consequences.

In the Japanese case, the extraordinarily negative attitudes toward the political leadership can be attributed directly to the scandals that wracked the ruling Liberal Democratic (Conservative) party during the two-year period in which this study was made. During that time the widespread political bribery case and a sexual scandal involving the prime minister himself forced the untimely resignations of two conservative prime ministers. The media was consumed with the revelations that nearly every major ruling conservative party leader was tainted by political bribery implicating big business interests. The amount of money involved reached enormous figures. The disclosures led to the first electoral defeat for political control, in the upper house only, for the conservatives in many decades. The negative reaction by the Japanese youth in our study reflected that of the society at large.

Parliamentary democracy has taken root in Japan, adapted to local customs and traditions. Party politics led by the conservatives thrives on political funds that, in an age of economic prosperity, require enormous amounts of money to keep the various competing internal factions loyal to the party itself. The excesses resulting in the huge amounts of funds in the gathering and dissemination of political contributions have reached scandalous proportions. Idealistic youth are consequently often turned off by the vulgarity of Japanese politics and its resulting influence on government.

Another predictable irony in these results is that although many of our outstanding students are quite critical of their government and political leaders, one of the main career routes into government service traditionally has been through the leading private secondary schools heavily represented in this survey. These prominent secondary schools have then led to Oxford and Cambridge, Tokyo and Kyoto Universities, and Harvard and Yale. From there the transition into the upper echelons of the respective governments has been smooth.

During the highly informative student interviews, a confusion arose concerning the distinction between the interpretation of "government" and "political" leaders. To the more sophisticated, government leaders identified high bureaucratic officials who run the day-to-day operations of the governmental machinery. The political leaders, on the other hand, are identified as those officials elected by the people to form the policies of the nation. The distinction between the two is more readily understood by the British and Japanese students where the governmental bureaucracy has established a separate identity. The Americans tend to view their political and governmental leaders as one and the same.

Regardless of the distinction between the two, or the lack of it, the results can be interpreted as a fairly widespread mistrust of the people who are associated in the minds of these young students with running their country. Politicians are seen by many as self-seeking individuals who make promises to their constituencies to get elected and reelected, but fail too often to follow through on them. Hopefully these negative responses may indicate that when this generation of future leaders ultimately arrives in leadership positions, they will serve their nation more responsibly.

The next series of questions touches upon various issues facing each of the three nations (see Question 19). The purpose is to determine how serious the future leaders perceive them as national problems.

Among the responses to these five diverse issues, two results are relatively similar while three are distinctly dissimilar. A deterioration of moral standards and protecting the natural environment are both considered serious national issues facing all three countries. A divergence among the other three topics, with the Japanese falling far short of both the

Question 19
Our country faces a serious problem with the following:

	Americans	British	Japanese
- The deterioration of moral standards -			
Agree	59.7%	43.9%	47.1%
Disagree	23.2	34.1	26.1
No opinion	16.0	21.8	25.1
- Drug use among youth -			
Agree	86.7	68.4	23.2
Disagree	6.3	16.9	47.8
No opinion	6.3	14.4	27.2
- Protecting the natural environment -			
Agree	85.8	81.0	78.5
Disagree	4.1	7.8	9.9
No opinion	8.5	10.8	10.1
- Academic standards of the schools -			
Agree	65.5	45.9	9.9
Disagree	20.3	32.0	60.8
No opinion	13.2	21.7	27.7
- The increasing number of immigrants coming into our country -			
Agree	30.3	43.6	7.6
Disagree	38.1	28.8	7.5
No opinion	30.8	27.2	23.0

Americans and the British, is evident with their attitudes toward academic standards, drug use, and immigrants.

Drug use among youth is considered a serious problem by only a minority of Japanese students (23%) in comparison to the British (68.4%) and Americans (86.7%). The differentiation is a reflection of the actual conditions. Drugs are not readily available in Japan, including the giant metropolitan areas. Consequently most Japanese students even in city schools seldom encounter their use, nor do they hear about a drug culture in their country. On the contrary, American and British youth are well aware of the widespread availability of drugs in their countries, especially in the major cities. American society in particular is portrayed as a drug culture throughout the media, in which the very capital of the country itself, Washington, D.C., is graphically portrayed as a city under siege in a nightly television program. This factor alone demonstrates that, although 47% of the Japanese believe that a deterioration of moral standards in their nation is a serious problem, in comparison to that of Britain and especially the United States, the actual severity of the problem is far less than perceived by the Japanese.

Few American youth can escape the daily media coverage of crime, violence, and drug abuse that pervades American society, so prominent within the cities. Our fairly sophisticated students participating in this project are all subjected to the dismal statistics about rising crime rates throughout American society. And yet a full 40% either disagree with, or have no opinion about, the statement concerning a deterioration of moral standards in the United States. Several students interviewed from the private sector felt that one reason for this response was that their boarding schools were located in pristine settings in rural America, far from the centers of crime, drug busts, and so on. Their daily lives were virtually divorced from such issues and consequently, although aware of them from the media, the students existed in an environment that exerted a strong effort to maintain decent standards of morality.

There is also a very large gap between Japan and the two Western countries over the issue of academic standards in the nation's schools. A healthy 65% of Americans recognize it as a problem for their country; 45.9% of the British also deem it a national problem. The Japanese are in the enviable position of only one in ten students perceiving academic standards as a national problem. Again the media in all three countries have given widespread coverage to the highly successful results of Japanese students on international achievement tests, as well as the severe educational problems confronting British and American schools in particular. But Japanese students are inescapably aware of the escalating demands of the university entrance examinations that have such a pervasive influence throughout the entire system.

Students from our outstanding schools in both Britain and America were quick to point out that they did not consider the academic standards of their own schools as deteriorating, but that of the nation's public schools as a whole. They virtually all felt that the academic demands and standards of their schools, which they recognize as outstanding, were probably now at the highest level. Only one American student dissented from this opinion; he felt that his private school's policy to diversify the student body by providing scholarships for minorities has brought the traditionally high academic standards of that school down somewhat. Still, there was no question in his mind that his school was academically outstanding.

These differing responses between our Eastern and Western students in themselves reflect one of the great divergencies in their national school systems, referred to previously. The university entrance examinations in Japan play an overriding role in determining academic standards for the entire system, not just for those students enrolled in the academically oriented schools such as those under review in this study. The entrance examinations can be described as the backbone of Japanese education, holding the academic standards from the first grade onward firmly in place. The university examinations in America and Britain do not play such a pivotal role in the entire school system; consequently they do not exert such broad influence on the educational standards throughout the school system. Our Western students recognize the great gulf between the academic standards of outstanding schools such as theirs, and the rest.

The other issue, immigration, also reveals a gap between Japan and the Western countries. Although illegal immigration is a major concern of the American government, more British students (43.6%) than American (30.3%) envision immigration as a serious national problem. The small number of Japanese (7.6%) who view it the same way reflects the fairly small number of immigrants entering the country annually. The high rate of British student concern is understandable in the context of the relatively small size of the country, which has already become one of the most ethnically diverse nations in the world. It also reflects the fact that an overwhelming majority of students enrolled in the outstanding schools participating in this poll are white, whereas the typical immigrant into Britain is not.

The very size of the United States makes it possible that a large number of our American respondents are not touched by the millions of illegal immigrants who flood the Texas and South Florida borders, spilling into city slums. Some of the outstanding schools in America are also currently undergoing a major social revolution, alluded to above, in the makeup of their student body to include a broader ethnic cross section originating from what is considered the immigrant community itself. This would naturally be reflected in a more sympathetic viewpoint toward immigrants than found in Britain, where our outstanding students especially in the private sector still have a great deal in common ethnically.

Although the ethnic transition has certainly not spread significantly to all of the private American schools in this study, the proportion of non-white students at our outstanding metropolitan public schools has increased sharply. For example, in one of our well-known city schools in the United States, over half of the student body is Asian. In one of our metropolitan public schools in Britain, many students obviously come from families that originated from the Indian subcontinent or the Caribbean area. In another distinguished private American school under study, a policy to diversify the student body from the traditionally white student has introduced significant numbers of black and Hispanic students to the campus on scholarships. Presumably many of these minority students who were surveyed would look more favorably upon American immigrants coming into the country.

A look at trade unions (see Questions 20, 21) certainly does not show an endorsement of the trade union movement in these three countries. In particular, over two-thirds of the British have little confidence in their trade unions. It should be recalled here that in the political spectrum, our future leaders place themselves more strongly toward the moderate to conservative position, a reflection no doubt of their family background. This sector of society is, in general, more critical of the labor movement than are those of a more liberal persuasion. It can be assumed that a relatively small percentage of the fathers of our students are members of trade unions.

The differences among the three nationalities correspond to the level of strikes called by unions in each country and the inconveniences the public experiences as a result of them. There has not been a labor strike of any import in Japan that our respondents could remember. To them militant labor unions are virtually an unknown quantity symbolized by the recent amalgamation of several major unions into a giant organization of moderate persuasion. There was no antagonism expressed toward unions by the Japanese students during the interviews. There was no support of them either.

Question 20
Trade unions in our country are too powerful.

	Americans	British	Japanese
Agree	16.5%	33.1%	4.6%
Disagree	22.0	37.5	56.5
No opinion	60.5	28.9	37.7

Question 21
How much confidence do you have in trade unions?

	Much	Some	Little
Americans	2.7%	58.6%	34.9%
British	3.2	30.6	65.3
Japanese	1.7	51.9	43.4

The geographical size of America, in comparison to Japan and Britain, tends to limit the effects of a union strike to a regional or localized area, thereby reducing the opportunities for a backlash against unions by the American students. Although of reduced frequency, striking unions in Britain, particularly in the transport sector, continue to sporadically disrupt public conveniences throughout the country. This militancy draws the wrath of the public in general, and the conservative government in particular. British students reflect a concern for union power that is able to mount such militant actions that affect their daily lives. Trade union militancy has received much media coverage throughout the lives of our British participants, evidenced during the interviews when several students expressed approval of the conservative government's attempt to curtail union power. Our American and Japanese students are much less aware of union activities in their country and therefore less negative toward the labor union movement in general.

The institutions of a nation from the backbone of the society. Our respondents will be dispersed throughout the various institutions, some public and others private, as they begin their careers within a few years, leading to positions of influence by the twenty-first century. Their attitudes toward their country's institutions can reveal how much confidence they have in the nation in general. Already we have seen how critical they are of their government leaders and their attitudes toward the trade union movement. We turn now to several other major institutions of the society.

Among the three, the Japanese have by far the least confidence in their military (see Question 22). Partly as a result of World War II and the brutalities of the Japanese armies, things associated with the military have not been popular among Japanese youth. The role and status of the Japanese army, navy, and air force have also been engulfed in controversy ever since the war. All Japanese students are exposed to the unique and controversial no-war clause in Japan's postwar constitution renouncing war as a means of solving disputes. The constitution specifically prohibits the formation of a Japanese army. To circumvent this constitutional restriction, the buildup of the Japanese military into one of the world's more modern and well-equipped armed services is sanctioned by the

Question 22
How much confidence do you have in the military?

	Much	Some	Little
Americans	27.5%	45.2%	26.9%
British	36.3	41.2	21.9
Japanese	3.3	27.5	68.0

ruling conservative party under the name of the *Jietai*, or Self-Defense Forces. The 68% of the future leaders of Japan are in essence expressing little confidence in this policy.

The British students exhibit the strongest degree of confidence in their military among the three groups, with 36% expressing much confidence, and only 21.9% little confidence in their armed services. Perhaps this should be compared with the American response of about one-fourth (27%) expressing much confidence in the American military establishment and about the same (26.9%) indicating little confidence in it. There are several factors underlying the differences, and one major factor explaining the great gulf between the two of them and Japan.

First of all, the differences between the Japanese and the British and Americans are most understandable. There is no question of the legitimacy and legality of the Western military forces. In addition their armies are not associated with foreign aggression or brutality as are the Japanese armies throughout Asia during World War II. Japanese youth are not exposed to the media protrayal of their courageous soldiers protecting the democratic way of life or the defense of the homeland, as are British and American youth not only by the media but through their textbooks as well. In a multiplicity of ways both American and British youth are exposed to their armed services, usually in a positive manner. The Japanese inevitably are not.

The one major exception involving a somewhat negative image of their armed services for American youth is the U.S. military involvement in Vietnam. Although this generation of American teenagers is several decades away from that distant war, they are still exposed to its brutalities, often wrought by the American forces, in the continual portrayal of "Nam" by American TV producers and film makers. It is not that far removed from this crop of teenagers, including the humiliating withdrawal of American forces from Vietnam essentially in defeat. It is, however, worth noting that the so-called Gulf War, which occurred just after the completion of this poll, may have erased many of the aftereffects of the Vietnam War.

There has also been a somewhat closer relationship between the British Public Schools, that is, private, and the British military officer corps than is found in the American tradition, although there has been one on a lesser scale in America. The so-called British establishment, analyzed in many books, outlines an intimate relationship between these private schools and the most influential sectors of the nation such as the monarchy, government bureaucracy, the BBC, the state church, and the military services, among others. The Public Schools, heavily represented in this research project, have thus traditionally supplied more than their share of the upper ranking British officer corps. Many of these prestigious schools also sponsor their own campus versions of a cadet corps that introduces students to military training, including visits to military bases, which make a deep impression on teenagers. No relationship exists between Japan's military establishment and its outstanding schools.

The role and prestige of each nation's major institutions for preparing its top officer corps is an additional factor in the overall image of the military among our respondents. West Point, Annapolis, and Sandhurst, for example, are highly respected institutions of higher learning in the United States and Britain, with impeccable credentials. They tradition- ally attract outstanding applicants, including those from our outstanding schools, who must pass rigorous academic and physical examinations, hopefully leading to the upper echelons of their respective military estab- lishments. To graduate from any of these institutions is a singular sign of distinction in the minds of the general public.

Conversely, the Boei Daigaku (Defense Academy), the West Point of Japan preparing this nation's career military officers, is virtually unknown to our students. To those who are aware of it, the institution has the image of a school for those who could not pass the entrance exami- nations to a regular university. In other words, its students are considered second-class in the pecking order. It has little appeal to students from our outstanding schools. This perception does not enhance the image of Japan's military establishment to the nation's future leaders.

The results of the study of military expenditures have implications for the future role of the military in the respective countries (see Question 23). To begin with Japan, the decision makers who have approved the controversial postwar military buildup are dominated by a generation of senior leaders who experienced World War II or the postwar threat of communist expansion in Asia, being surrounded by the two communist giants, China and the Soviet Union. The specter of communist armies in- vading Japan, with a Soviet military base located just a few miles north of Japan on a disputed island chain formerly under Japanese control, has haunted the nation's leaders ever since the war. Although this poll extended into the era of the remarkable dissolution of Western European communist supremacy, those developments had not yet noticeably influ- enced the Asian scene, with an intransigent leadership in China and

Question 23
Our country should increase military expenditures.

	Americans	British	Japanese
Agree	8.3%	13.6%	8.1%
Disagree	76.9	63.4	76.6
No opinion	14.2	22.5	13.4

North Korea maintaining a hard-line communist policy. Nevertheless this generation of future Japanese leaders has a different perception of the importance of the Japanese military which may portend a less favorable attitude toward Japan's defense forces in the twenty-first century.

Although there is a considerably more positive attitude toward the military among British and American youth than among Japanese youth, there is no strong vote of confidence among them either. This sentiment may also portend a more moderate approach to further expansion of the military in these two countries as well. As in Japan, the threat of communist expansion has played a major role in gaining approval for large military budgets in both Britain and America. With that threat perceived as subsiding ever so rapidly with the collapse of European communism, the twenty-first-century leaders indicate that, as in Japan, the American and British miltary power should be diminished.

Moderation prevails in the perception of the media (see Question 24). One might call it a skeptical attitude with a majority, or near majority, in every possible choice falling in the middle category of the cautious "some confidence." Overall, the Americans show the strongest confidence in the media and the British the least. With the Americans, greatest confidence comes with newspapers, attributed in part by the students themselves to the localized nature and coverage of the American newspaper industry. Among the three countries, America is the only one without a truly national newspaper equivalent to the *Times* of Britain or the *Asahi Shimbun* of Japan.

The British students stand out as most critical of newspapers. The so-called sensational press in Britain plays a much more prominent role in the printed media than in America or Japan, in which exaggeration and hyperbole are stretched beyond credulity. Although Fleet Street, traditional home of British newspapers until recently, is renowned for responsible reporting through the serious press, the racy modern tabloids have captured a significant share of the newspaper market. These sophisticated students react accordingly. The believability and respectability of the

Question 24
How much confidence do you have in newspapers and television?

(Newspapers/Television)

	Much	Some	Little
Americans	24.2%/12.9%	61.8%/56.2%	13.4%/30.3%
British	3.9 /8.9	49.8 /65.0	46.0 /25.5
Japanese	18.2 /8.9	67.7 /68.7	13.3 /21.4

American and Japanese press produce more confidence in them by the young.

There is a convergence at a fairly high level of criticism of the television medium by all three groups, ranging from 21.4% of the Japanese registering little confidence in it, up to the high of 30.3% by the Americans. The category of much confidence attracted only about 10% from each group. Since television plays a powerful role, so we are told, in the formation of public opinion in all three countries, and our future leaders will be playing a significant role in determining its direction in the twenty-first century, this cautious reaction to it may be a positive influence for the future. Although our interviewees claim their image of, and attitudes toward, other peoples are formed primarily from television coverage, their skepticism of what they see and hear through the information media in general could render them more responsible and deliberate decision makers.

In all three countries the public schools have come under criticism for a variety of reasons, and students express varying degrees of censure per country over such issues as violence, drugs, and a deterioration of academic standards, among others (see Question 25). Even in Japan the issue of classroom or school violence provoked national concern during the period of this study, although in comparison the actual discipline problems in Japanese schools were far fewer than those confronted by American and British teachers and administrators. Nevertheless there is general discontent among the public about the schools in all three countries including Japan, where criticism over the state of Japanese education abounds. Much of that criticism is focused on the overwhelming influence of university examination preparation on the education of the future

Question 25
How much confidence do you have in your public schools?

	Much	Some	Little
Americans	19.3%	60.1%	19.9%
British	17.1	60.0	22.2
Japanese	13.0	66.9	19.3

In your nation's universities?

	Much	Some	Little
Americans	53.7%	43.6%	2.0%
British	48.7	45.8	4.7
Japanese	10.3	69.7	17.9

leaders in these select schools under study. Paradoxically, these schools would not be included in this study if they did not emphasize examination preparation, an indication that little will be done to meet the criticisms.

The question concerning confidence in universities proved quite interesting because it divides the three groups once again basically into two, the East and the West. What makes this division somewhat unusual is that preparation for, and entry into, the finest universities in the land is the overriding purpose of both these students and the outstanding schools in which they are currently enrolled in all three countries. If there is one factor these 3,000 students from Europe, North America, and Asia have in common, it is university preparation. And yet their attitudes are sharply divided about that institution they are all devoting so much effort to enter.

The major difference is seen in the wide gap of only 10% of Japanese students who have much confidence in universities, versus about half of both the American and British students, who have the most positive perceptions. To the casual observer, this would appear incongruous. Tokyo, Kyoto, Keio, and Waseda Universities, for example, typical of the schools so many of our Japanese respondents enter, are as famous in Japan as Oxford and Cambridge, and Harvard and Yale are in Britain and America, respectively. And yet few Japanese students who will be entering these elite universities express strong confidence in them. Nearly one in five have little confidence in the university system they aspire to enter.

The discrepancy is nevertheless quite understandable. The major universities in America and England are internationally recognized as not only academically stimulating but also academically demanding. The entering student expects to be challenged by the university. In turn, the student fully expects to receive a university education that will enable him to secure a career position leading to a responsible post. Many confidently expect their university education to enable them to ultimately become leaders in their field of endeavor.

The Japanese university does not inspire much confidence in the entering student because, in general, it is not academically stimulating or demanding. The most common adage describing the Japanese university scene—extremely difficult to enter but easy to graduate from—is not only apt, it is a desciption that does not inspire strong confidence. It is, rather, a devastating critique of the Japanese higher education system. The public at large is well aware of this peculiar aspect of Japanese education; so are the students.

All students know that, except for a very few subjects, the academic requirements to graduate from any Japanese university are notoriously minimal. Student absenteeism is rampant among universities, including the most prestigious, where students are confident they can pass the course examinations with no great effort required just prior to the examination period. Reading assignments, paper requirements, and so forth, are minimal if existent at all. Although student confidence in Japanese universities is not high in comparison to that of their Western peers, their expectation of graduating successfully once they enter is nearly complete since very few fail on academic grounds. All students, as well as their parents and the university faculty, are fully aware of this phenomenon of the Japanese university system. It clearly does not inspire confidence in the institution.

Japanese secondary students, enrolled in the major university preparatory schools that characterize every one of them in this survey, also realize that it is not their university course of study or their course grades that will prepare them for a good position in their future career. It is, rather, the name and reputation of the university that is the primary factor in securing employment with a well-known company leading to a responsible career position. Moreover students are also confident that they will be given the opportunity to learn the skills and knowledge necessary for a successful career not from their four years at the university but through the training program set up by their employer after graduation. American and British students confidently expect to receive basic career preparation to a considerable extent from their university course.

The final question in this chapter (Question 26) was designed as a general summary of the attitudes and perceptions of the future leaders toward their country. It was included after the respondents had gone through the list of potential problems such as pollution, drugs, and the deterioration of moral standards, all of which are unavoidable issues to some degree in every country. It should also be recalled that these respondents in all three countries are sitting at or near the pinnacle of academic success as students in the outstanding secondary schools in their country. And, finally, at the time of the survey, all three countries, led by Japan, had experienced an unprecedented period of economic stability or growth. The respondents in our survey have never knowingly experienced the effects of a severe economic crisis in their country.

Question 26
In general, are you satisfied with the way things are going in your country today?

	Americans	British	Japanese
Very well satisfied	2.6%	3.4%	1.8%
Satisfied	43.0	47.0	31.9
Dissatisfied	43.1	36.3	43.6
Very dissatisfied	9.7	12.7	21.6

Under the economic conditions described above, the few students in each country who said they are very well satisfied with the way things are going in their country may be surprising. However, combining the two satisfied categories, we see that 45% of the Americans, 50% of the British, and just over 33% of the Japanese are generally satisfied with the way things are going in their country. This is a far lower percentage than found on the question from the previous chapter when the students were asked about the way things are going in their life today, a very personal query. Question 27 makes the comparison.

There is obviously a certain dilemma for the students in responding to these two separate but interrelated questions. They have witnessed the relative economic prosperity in their countries, highly noticeable in Japan, of course. Yet they all are aware of the enormous problems their societies face with the spread of drugs, environmental pollution, and other issues that vary somewhat from country to country. Nevertheless, in all three countries these students also have a high degree of confidence in entering a good to superior university and eventually obtaining good to superior employment.

There is also a degree of irony in the fact that, among the three groups of participants, the Japanese students are the most dissatisfied with the way things are going in their country. Yet it is Japan that has experienced the fastest growth rates and the most impressive economic performance among the three countries. In spite of their accomplishments as a nation, the Japanese youth remain considerably more critical of conditions within their country than do the Americans or British. Rather than boasting, they criticize. Even though they sit patiently in class taking voluminous notes in preparation for the university entrance examinations, underneath that passive exterior Japan's future leaders harbor perceptions that circumstances within their country are far from satisfactory.

Again, a sense of modesty enters into the picture, coupled with a hard-headed reality characteristic of the Japanese that can only be appreciated from within the society. It is a perspective that helps shape the Japanese attitudes toward themselves and others. It cannot be overstated that, in

Question 27
Are you satisfied with the way things are going

	(Yes/No)		
	Americans	British	Japanese
In your country today?	45.6%/52.8%	50.4%/49.0%	33.7%/65.2%
In your life today?	84.3 /14.4	81.6 /17.7	50.4 /48.3

Source: Questions 4 and 26 revised.

school and out, the lack of space, the overcrowdedness and all that accompanies it such as the lack of leisure facilities, affects virtually every aspect of life in Japan from the cradle to the grave. The curious but perfectly understandable practice of placing the ashes from mandatory cremation of the deceased in jars on tiny grave plots or even lined up on shelves in special buildings is a vivid example of how this nation must accommodate the lack of space.

This generation has been brought up amidst prosperity, so they are told by an older generation that experienced either wartime or the postwar depression. But they are constantly reminded just how restrictive that prosperity remains with unbelievably crowded trains, a dearth of open spaces, and the cramped living conditions in general. What is understood by the Japanese, and particularly by the caliber of students involved in this study, is that Japan is a small country chronically short of land, supporting a large population. Teachers often refer to Japan as a small or narrow country, which it is. That attitude permeates the psyche of each generation.

Ironically, the vast majority of the Japanese consider themselves middle class when polled on the subject, which is often in this nation experiencing high growth rates. But one of the reasons for this response is simply that few Japanese would classify themselves as lower class. They are too highly educated, literate, and proud to characterize themselves as poor lower-class citizens. The near-absence of city slums places the entire population somewhere above the lower socioeconomic levels. But this huge middle-class society understands that to live an American-style middle-class life, with which they inevitably compare their own, requires an upper-class income in Japan. Consequently many of our students do not feel they are sharing adequately in Japan's newly gained prosperity.

Compounding the all-embracing influence of the geogaphical realities of Japan is the enormous personal burden of academic pressure placed upon our students, who have run the gauntlet of university preparation. Add to this mixture the long-running expose of political corruption that has mired the ruling conservative party in unseemly scandals, and you have a combination of factors explaining the reason why 65% of our Japanese youth are dissatisfied with the way things are going in their country today. They may have reached the lofty heights of educational success at their age level, but it has been at a high personal price of self-sacrifice under difficult conditions.

It is appropriate now to turn from how these students perceive their own country and people to how they perceive the other countries and their peoples involved in this study. Through their perceptions of others we can also gain some additional insights into their perceptions of themselves and their country as they prepare for leadership roles in the twenty-first century.

4

PERCEPTIONS OF EACH OTHER

Creative—Industrious—Individualistic

Our outstanding secondary school students from America, Britain, and Japan, destined for leadership positions in the twenty-first century, will eventually become influential in developing policy toward each other. It is, therefore, of considerable concern to ascertain how each of the three groups perceives the others. A list of various traits was drawn up, similar to those used in the previous chapter, in which each group of 1,000 students was asked to evaluate each of the other two nationalities on a continuum from very positive to negative. The results enable us, then, to make a multiple evaluation by comparing how each group feels about the others. We also, by referring to the previous chapter, can compare not only how they feel about each other, but how those perceptions of other people compare with the perceptions each holds about their own people.

The most notable results from Table 10 show that the American image of the Japanese falls primarily into two categories: highly industrious (69.1%) and highly intelligent (61%). This differs noticeably from the American student image of their fellow Americans, who were, as seen in Table 11, characterized as highly industrious by only 16.9% and highly intelligent by 23.1%. This exemplifies, to be sure, a very positive perception of the Japanese people in qualities greatly admired by Americans. It reflects an indirect recognition of the new status Japan has gained as an economic superpower.

Juxtaposed in this manner (Table 11), the consistency in the very highest category of 5 on both industriousness and intelligence is rather remarkable, not only in the very positive impression our American

Table 10
American student perception of the Japanese

	Not very				Highly
	1	2	3	4	5
Creative	9.0%	16.3%	24.7%	22.5%	21.1%
Loyal	1.2	3.1	13.2	21.6	55.0
Emotional	17.8	28.6	27.9	11.0	8.0
Materialistic	4.9	14.6	30.2	23.9	19.7
Individualistic	22.7	30.4	22.0	10.2	7.3
Industrious	0.6	1.1	4.6	17.8	69.1
Generous	7.4	15.6	45.5	16.7	7.8
Trustworthy	4.0	7.8	36.8	27.4	16.7
Polite	2.7	4.4	14.8	26.8	45.0
Forgiving	7.0	17.9	42.2	17.3	7.8
Aggressive	4.5	9.7	22.5	26.0	30.6
Intelligent	0.7	0.5	6.6	25.0	61.0

Table 11
American student perception of industriousness and intelligence

	Not very			Highly		
			- Industrious -			
	1	2	3	4	5	(4+5)
Americans	1.8%	8.2%	30.1%	35.7%	16.9%	(52.6%)
Japanese	0.6	1.1	4.6	17.8	69.1	(86.9)
			- Intelligent -			
Americans	2.0	4.3	23.6	40.6	23.1	(63.7)
Japanese	0.7	0.5	6.6	25.0	61.0	(86.0)

Source: Excerpted from Tables 7 and 10.

students have of the Japanese, but also in the lower opinion they have of Americans. The interviews, however, revealed an ambiguity in their perceptions. To these future leaders of America, the Japanese people are envisioned as more industrious and intelligent than the American public at large, but not necessarily more so than these outstanding American students themselves. In fact there was an underlying attitude of superiority revealed through nuances and asides, expressed from one American to another in conversation held within the familiar surroundings of the students' schools, detected throughout the interviews.

Although the American students who participated in this study indicated a very positive image of the Japanese people, there was nevertheless in private a persistent undertone tinged with a degree of arrogance that the Japanese were not yet on an equal footing with Americans. This characteristic of the American personality is evident in the negotiations between the contemporary leaders of the two nations over trade policies. The position taken by the American side is that the Japanese must be taught a lesson through forceful words and actions before they will respond, similar to a teacher-student relationship. American leaders do not take that attitude, for example, toward the French over their refusal to join in the American-led military pact for Western Europe in the postwar era. Even though the French have been as frustrating to the Americans as the Japanese at various times, American leaders do not harbor a superiority complex toward the French, as they indicate in indirect and not-so-indirect ways toward the Japanese. The future leaders of America have to a certain degree already formed such an attitude, which will most likely be carried over into the twenty-first century.

On the negative side in Table 10, the very lowest percentage in the highly category, number 5, came under highly individualistic, with only 7.3% of the Americans holding that image of the Japanese. What makes this somewhat significant is that individualism is a trait cherished and admired by Americans. This result also mirrors an image of the Japanese long held by foreigners and by the Japanese people themselves, since only 17.6% of Japanese youth describe their own people as highly individualistic, shown in Table 9. At the opposite end, not very individualistic, represented the highest percentage (22.7%) chosen by the Americans about the Japanese under number 1. This reinforces a negative image of the Japanese in terms of one of the most highly regarded characteristics of Americans by Americans, and may underlie that superiority complex toward the Japanese that apparently lies just beneath the surface of the American personality.

With some justification Americans traditionally envisioned the Japanese as imitators exploiting other peoples' ideas, mainly American as the thinking goes, by cleverly improving on the original. This demonstrated to Americans that the Japanese could not be recognized as creative

people. However, this historical image may finally be undergoing altera-
tion with one in five (21.1%) perceiving the Japanese as highly creative.
Adding the two most positive categories of 4 and 5 together, fully 43.6%
of the American students describe the Japanese as creative. Only 9%
chose the most negative "not very creative" response.

Another historical image of the Japanese appears to be diminishing. An
older generation of Americans experienced, or were brought up to regard
the Japanese people as perfidious, exemplified by the so-called sneak
attack on Pearl Harbor. They were people who could not be trusted. The
current generation of American youth indicates a different attitude is
emerging, with 16.7% describing the Japanese as highly trustworthy (see
Table 12). Further, adding the two positive categories of 4 and 5 together,
44.1% place the Japanese in this most significant position as trustworthy.
Only 4% of the American students believe the Japanese are not very
trustworthy.

For comparative purposes, only 9.9% of our American participants
believe their fellow countrymen are highly trustworthy. Adding categories 4 and 5 together about Americans by Americans, the total of 32.8%
still falls considerably short of the 44.1% for the Japanese. When
compared in this manner, these future leaders of America have a more
positive image of the Japanese people in terms of trustworthiness than
they do of their own people. It would appear that the image of the Japanese by contemporary American youth reflects a new postwar perception
that corresponds with Japan's recently acquired status in world affairs.

One of the most striking differences between the American perception
of the Japanese and the Japanese perception of themselves falls within the
trait of aggressiveness, worthy of some consideration (see Table 13). A
majority of 56.6% of the American students consider the Japanese aggressive, combining the two highest categories of 4 and 5 from Table 10. In
sharp contrast only 12% of the Japanese students characterize themselves
as aggressive, shown in Table 9 using the same measure. There are several
aspects involved in these findings. First of all an older generation of
Americans usually thought of the Japanese as aggressive in military terms

Table 12
American student perception of trustworthiness

	Not very				Highly	
	1	2	3	4	5	(4+5)
Japanese	4.0%	7.8%	36.8%	27.4%	16.7%	(44.1%)
Americans	4.3	15.5	40.8	22.9	9.9	(32.8)

Table 13

American and Japanese perception of Japanese as aggressive people

	Not very				Highly
	1	2	3	4	5
Americans	4.5%	9.7%	22.5%	26.0	30.6%
Japanese	16.2	38.0	31.9	7.9	4.1

Source: Excerpted from Tables 9 and 10.

as a result of World War II. But this generation, as revealed in the many interviews, holds a different understanding of aggressiveness when applied to the Japanese. The future leaders of America perceive the Japanese as highly aggressive not as soldiers but as businessmen. In this sense the image takes on a certain positive value to them since a common attitude within the capitalistic framework of American society is that the successful businessman must be aggressive. The contemporary Japanese epitomize that image to this generation of Americans, replacing that of the militarily aggressive Japanese of the past.

The Japanese, in sharp contrast, perceive themselves as not very aggressive (Table 9), with a majority of 54.2% choosing categories 1 and 2. Although 62.7% also consider the Japanese highly industrious, that does not imply to them that their industrious people are aggressive. There are cultural and linguistic patterns of the society that influence this perception. For example, even the most aggressive Japanese businessman, in the American sense, would exhibit in public a demeanor of politeness in speech and reticence in manner. The image of the successful Japanese businessman to many of our youthful Japanese respondents is one of polite modesty. It runs counter to that of the Japanese businessman held by the Americans.

To summarize, then, the most positive images of the Japanese by the American students far outweigh the most negative aspects, which fall in the two categories of not very individualistic (22.7%) and not very emotional (17.8%). The most positive categories of industrious (69.1%) and intelligent (61%) represent traits that Americans tend to admire. This positive image derives, in part, from the close familiarity with, and virtual dependency on, Japanese products in the everyday life of American youth. It also stems from the immense amount of publicity given to the international test scores in which Japanese students consistently outperform American students in various subject-matter tests.

These attitudes tend to strengthen youthful American confidence in

Japanese products, giving the made-in-Japan or the made-in-America Japanese brand a significant boost in the highly competitive American domestic markets, fueling the imbalances of trade between the two countries that have become the major source of bilateral friction. If patterns of personal growth and development follow the course cited by researchers in Chapter 1, the current attitudes held by our future American leaders will to a great extent be carried with them into the twenty-first century. That scenario is not a positive one for the American government officials endeavoring to reduce the huge trade imbalances with Japan.

In general, no characteristic of the British stands out for the Americans in either the highest or the lowest categories (see Table 14). There are simply no extremes in the image of the British by the Americans. In this regard it is remarkably similar to the image of the British by the British teenagers themselves, as shown in the previous chapter, Table 8. Only on

Table 14
American student perception of the British

	Not very				Highly
	1	2	3	4	5
Creative	2.5%	11.1%	49.8%	25.3%	8.4%
Loyal	0.9	4.4	32.6	35.2	18.8
Emotional	4.0	10.0	37.2	30.7	9.4
Materialistic	0.7	5.8	37.9	35.7	11.2
Individualistic	1.2	7.6	37.0	33.1	12.2
Industrious	1.6	11.0	47.5	27.0	3.8
Generous	2.6	9.2	46.3	26.3	6.9
Trustworthy	1.4	4.7	37.2	34.1	13.6
Polite	3.3	7.1	22.5	30.8	27.3
Forgiving	1.6	7.2	46.6	26.9	8.0
Aggressive	2.6	16.7	45.1	20.5	5.4
Intelligent	1.5	4.0	31.3	40.3	14.0

one trait does there appear any sizable response either in the not very (1) or highly (5) categories. Curiously 27.3% of the Americans consider the British highly polite. Other than that, the results fall primarily down the middle.

We are now, however, able to compare the American perception of the British, traditional Western allies with whom Americans share much in common, with their perception of the Japanese, their modern allies from Asia. The contrast is sharp. Using category 5 (highly) as our first measure, the trait that attracted the highest percentage vis-à-vis the Japanese, highly industrious with 69.1%, drew the very lowest number, 3.8%, in describing the British. The second highest trait concerning the Japanese, highly intelligent (61%), attracted only 14% for the British. In addition, only 8.4% considered the British highly creative in comparison to 21.1% ascribing that quality to the Japanese. The contrast between the image of America's historical ally, not to mention its mother country, and the new postwar ally of the Japanese appears quite pronounced.

We are also now in the position not only of being able to compare the attitudes of the future leaders of America toward the British and the Japanese; we have sufficient data to make a three-way comparison to include Americans themselves (see Table 15). Among the more prominent results, the traits of creativeness, industriousness, and individualism attract attention. To the Americans, their fellow countrymen remain the most creative, followed by the Japanese. The British take a distant third position. Concerning industriousness, the Japanese are clearly in a class by themselves with the British falling even further behind their ranking than with creativity. However, when it comes to individualism, the tables are turned. The American students rank their own people far out in front, followed by the British. The Japanese in this instance take a distant third position, with the historical image of the Japanese as group-oriented being more firmly established in the American mind.

The final comparison of some interest from the basic Table 14 concerns intelligence. American students, especially in these outstanding schools, receive a rather strong dose of English literature during the course of their studies. Shakespeare is required reading for all. In addition, Dickens and several other British writers are also well known to these students. From more modern times, British leaders such as Winston Churchill and his inspiring speeches are familiar to the majority of our American students in this study. In other words the British have played a role in American history and education that no other nation or people have, and it has been to an overwhelming extent favorable. American textbooks are full of famous British figures.

American textbooks are certainly not replete with famous Japanese figures worthy of respect to compare with Shakespeare in the literary field or Churchill in the political arena. Just the opposite is true. And yet this

Table 15
American student perception of creativity, industriousness, and individualism

	Not very				Highly
- Creative -					
	1	2	3	4	5
Americans	1.4%	3.7%	17.7%	39.1%	31.8%
British	2.5	11.1	49.8	25.3	8.4
Japanese	9.0	16.3	24.7	22.5	21.1
- Industrious -					
Americans	1.8	8.2	30.1	35.7	16.9
British	1.6	11.0	47.5	27.0	3.8
Japanese	0.6	1.1	4.6	17.8	69.1
- Individualistic -					
Americans	1.3	4.7	15.0	27.1	45.6
British	1.2	7.6	37.0	33.1	12.2
Japanese	22.7	30.4	22.0	10.2	7.3

Source: Excerpted from Tables 7, 10, and 14.

generation of Americans considers the Japanese the most intelligent among the three nationalities. Comparing category 5 (Table 10) under the heading of highly intelligent, 61% of the American respondents describe the Japanese as highly intelligent, 31% believe Americans are highly intelligent (Table 7), with only 23.1% placing the British in the same category (Table 14). Against rather severe odds, the Japanese have attained a remarkably high standing as intelligent people in comparison to the British and the Americans as perceived by Americans themselves.

The strongest images (category 5) of the American people held by our Japanese teenagers (see Table 16) are highly emotional (49.1%), highly individualistic (45.8%), and highly aggressive (44.5%), resembling the image of Americans by American teenagers themselves, as analyzed previously. The major difference falls within the emotional trait, in which the Japanese perceive the Americans in far stronger terms. Consid-

Table 16
Japanese student perception of Americans

	Not very				Highly
	1	2	3	4	5
Creative	3.4%	2.9%	11.6%	37.8%	41.6%
Loyal	12.6	25.0	37.7	12.8	9.4
Emotional	2.7	3.4	13.6	28.1	49.1
Materialistic	2.8	5.4	33.6	28.7	26.1
Individualistic	3.0	4.1	19.0	24.7	45.8
Industrious	10.5	26.3	43.7	13.1	2.6
Generous	5.0	7.3	38.6	31.7	14.3
Trustworthy	9.1	15.6	45.8	21.0	5.6
Polite	11.3	20.4	46.0	16.2	2.7
Forgiving	8.1	11.1	33.5	25.4	18.8
Aggressive	1.7	2.0	15.9	33.2	44.5
Intelligent	6.9	14.2	50.2	21.7	4.3

ering the fact that the Japanese characteristically gravitate toward the middle ground in responding to inquiries, the result of nearly half choosing the most extreme category of 5 on a scale from 1 to 5 indicated a particularly strong image of Americans as emotional, individualistic, and aggressive.

This perception can be attributed in part to the influence of the portrayal of Americans as aggressive, often violent, in the constant run of American films and TV programs available in Japan. In addition the daily news devoted to international coverage is a prolific source of events out of America that often depict Americans as both aggressive and individualistic. The massive military response to the oil crisis in the Middle East by the American government represents an example of the image of the Americans spread around the world as both aggressive and individualistic, with American forces taking the leading role in the so-called Gulf War. The John Wayne syndrome is associated with the American character in the Japanese mind as it is in the American mentality.

Recent events also underscore the highly aggressive nature of Americans in their relations with the Japanese, exhibiting strong emotional overtones. The so-called Japan bashing by outspoken Americans especially in industry and labor, in reaction to the perceived closed domestic markets of Japan to American products, is a constant illustration to the Japanese public of American aggressiveness. Japanese tend to sublimate their aggressive inclinations through indirect language obscuring their true feelings, or by revealing them only behind the scenes in a nonpublic manner. The openness and directness of American criticisms of Japan especially in the area of trade and commerce on which Japan depends is particularly viewed as aggressive emotional behavior by the Japanese generally unaccustomed to such tactics in their social patterns.

The other area where American aggressiveness is marked indelibly on the Japanese psyche is in military affairs. The American position articulated not only by military leaders but also by politicians and the industrial circles associated with military production has been characterized throughout the 1980s by a provocative posture. The enormous pressure on Japan to increase its military strength guarding against communist expansion in East Asia has been a constant theme until only very recently, pervading American policy toward Japan. The strong rhetoric, which has implied that Japan has been enjoying a free ride in military defense at the expense of the American taxpayer ever since the end of the war, has been viewed by the future leaders of Japan as highly aggressive. It contrasts sharply with the conduct of Japanese foreign affairs in a manner that was once thought even in America as, ironically, diplomatic.

The recent spate of Japan bashing, particularly in commerce and trade, underlies the strong trait attributed to Americans as highly emotional (49.1%). The outbursts of criticism and the severity of the language employed is, to the Japanese, indicative of deep emotionalism running through the American character. Again the contrast must be seen with the Japanese character, where the control of one's personal feelings in public is held with deep respect. Consequently when a Japanese loses self-control with impetuous bursts of emotional feelings, it exerts a strong impact. It is from this perception that the young Japanese view the American outbursts of criticism of Japan as both aggressive and emotional, two traits not held in high esteem within Japanese society.

Surprisingly only one in four (26.1%) perceive Americans as highly materialistic, the third major trait Americans ascribe to themselves, and one that traditionally has been associated with the United States as the major consuming society in the modern world. The Japanese, rather, have replaced the Americans in their own minds as a materialistic society, with 42.9% describing the Japanese people as highly materialistic, considered in the previous chapter. The fact that each group perceives its own society as more materialistic than the other is in itself a commentary on modern societies experiencing long periods of economic expansion (see Table 17). What makes it most impressive with the Japanese situation is that they began, in effect, from ground zero, near total economic destruction at war's end in 1945, achieving the dubious status as materialistic in less than half a century.

Among the traits that can be considered in the most negative terms by these outstanding Japanese youth in their perception of Americans are highly industrious (2.6%) and highly intelligent (5.5%) under category 5 (Table 16). At the opposite end, combining the two most negative categories of 1 (10.5%) and 2 (26.3%), over a third of Japanese youth (36.8%) believe the Americans are not very industrious. This compares with combining the two most positive categories of 4 and 5 for a total of only 15.7% describing Americans as highly industrious. It also compares most unfavorably with the very positive response of 71.5% of the Japanese and 69.1% of the Americans who consider the Japanese as highly industrious under the most extreme category of number 5 only.

The other fairly negative response falls under the trait of intelligence, where only 4.3% of the Japanese consider Americans highly intelligent (category 5). Even combining categories 4 and 5, it adds up to only 26% holding a positive image of American intelligence. Again the contrast with the American image of the Japanese as highly intelligent (61%) and not very intelligent (0.7%) is extreme. On this most acute trait of intelligence, the image of the two groups of teenagers toward each other is virtually opposite (see Table 18).

The Japanese are exposed to the many reports emanating from America about the high rates of illiteracy among American adults and the criticism

Table 17
Japanese and American student perception of materialism

	Not very				Highly	
	1	2	3	4	5	(4 + 5)

— Japanese students —

| Japanese | 1.5% | 5.3% | 15.8% | 31.9% | 42.9% | (74.8%) |
| Americans | 2.8 | 5.4 | 33.6 | 28.7 | 26.1 | (54.8) |

— American students —

| Japanese | 4.9% | 14.6% | 32.2% | 23.9% | 19.7% | (43.6%) |
| Americans | 0.5 | 0.3 | 4.9 | 22.8 | 65.6 | (88.4) |

Source: Excerpted from Tables 9 and 16.

Table 18
Japanese and American student perception of intelligence

	Not very				Highly	
	1	2	3	4	5	(4 + 5)
Japanese of Americans	6.9%	14.2%	50.2%	21.7%	4.3%	(26.0%)
Americans of Japanese	0.7	0.5	6.6	24.0	61.0	(85.0)

Source: Excerpted from Tables 10 and 16.

of American schools over the grave problems of high dropout rates, school violence, academic standards, and so on. In addition, the widely reported results of international studies of achievements in mathematics and other subjects, mentioned previously, in which Japanese students perpetually score at or near the top and American students much lower, sometimes at or near the bottom, cast doubt on American academic standards among the Japanese.

On the other hand, the Japanese perception of their own people as intelligent falls considerably short of the image of them held by the Americans. For example, a strong majority of 61% of the Americans consider the Japanese people highly intelligent. In contrast only 21.6% of the Japanese students have the same opinion of their own people. The opposite is shown with the Japanese impression of American intelligence. Only 4.3% of our Japanese respondents believe that Americans are highly intelligent. In contrast, 23.1% of our American respondents believe that their fellow Americans are highly intelligent. Once again an element of modesty on the part of the Japanese participants would underlie the more cautious attitudes about themselves.

Another result of some interest concerns the Japanese perception of Americans in terms of creativeness. One often encounters in Japan itself the criticism of the Japanese as not being creative, and Americans as being very creative. This study substantiates that continuing attitude, with an overwhelming number of Japanese youth (4 + 5: 79.9%) perceiving Americans as creative in contrast to only 25.4% (categories 4 + 5) of them holding the Japanese in the same image (see Table 19). The American student image of creativeness among the two peoples falls in the same direction although the differences are not as extreme.

The next table presents the Japanese image of the British, using identical traits (see Table 20). From these results we are able to determine if there are major differences between the Japanese image of two Western peoples with whom they have close historical, cultural, and economic

Table 19
Japanese and American student perception of creativity

	Not very				Highly	
	1	2	3	4	5	(4 + 5)

- Japanese students -

	1	2	3	4	5	(4 + 5)
Japanese	19.9%	29.8%	23.3%	15.9%	9.5%	(25.4%)
Americans	3.4	2.9	11.6	37.8	41.6	(79.4)

- American students -

	1	2	3	4	5	(4 + 5)
Japanese	9.0%	16.3%	24.7%	22.5%	21.1%	(43.6%)
Americans	1.4	3.7	17.7	39.1	31.8	(70.9)

Source: Excerpted from Tables 9 and 16.

Table 20
Japanese student perception of the British

	Not very				Highly
	1	2	3	4	5
Creative	4.0%	9.8%	44.8%	28.3%	10.2%
Loyal	4.6	7.8	37.6	32.7	14.6
Emotional	4.8	14.9	41.2	25.8	9.7
Materialistic	4.0	9.2	50.5	25.5	9.3
Individualistic	2.9	4.8	31.4	34.7	22.9
Industrious	4.5	8.7	46.5	30.2	6.3
Generous	3.5	5.5	38.8	33.0	16.0
Trustworthy	6.0	6.6	40.2	32.7	11.4
Polite	2.7	4.0	22.1	35.5	32.4
Forgiving	4.0	10.3	41.6	29.4	11.2
Aggressive	5.1	15.7	46.9	20.5	8.3
Intelligent	2.8	4.1	27.9	40.4	21.6

ties, as well as linguistic relationships since English is the major foreign language studied by all students in school and out.

The Japanese students have had very little direct or indirect contact with the British, in comparison to their exposure to Americans and American society and customs in a variety of forms. Therefore their perception of the British is a distant one, although the two nations have pursued close diplomatic and cultural relationships. The image of the British is oftentimes related to the royal family portrayed in ceremonial events, contrasting sharply with the image of Americans as viewed in the Hollywood versions of films that are such an important part of the Japanese cinema. The imperial Japanese family has, in the modern period, expressed a certain affinity for the British royal family. The medieval universities of Oxford and Cambridge are also venerable institutions to the Japanese, who have encountered them in textbooks and often on television. Pointedly, the crown prince was sent for overseas study to Oxford rather than an Amerian university. The image of the British by our Japanese teenagers must be seen from this limited perspective. Nevertheless Japanese industry has targeted Britain for major investments, thereby gaining access to the forthcoming united European Community. Their image of the British, consequently, is of growing concern and interest to both countries.

In general, the image of the British people as seen by the Japanese is a positive one. No negative response in the not very category of 1 reached higher than 6%. On the other hand the highest positive category of 5 was registered in the highly polite image by only 32.4%. This relates rather closely to the most vivid picture of the British in terms of royalty with their formalistic rituals and polite language. This style would be considered very polite form in Japanese society, somewhat reminiscent of the extremely polite subtleties of the Japanese imperial family.

The next strongest trait of the British chosen by the Japanese is highly individualistic (22.9%), followed by highly intelligent (21.6%). Although neither of these attributes runs into significant percentages, when the two top positive categories are added, that is, 4 and 5, the combined results are quite impressive: highly individualistic—57.6%, and highly intelligent—62%. The comparable figures (4 + 5) for the Japanese image of Americans are highly individualistic—70.5%, and highly intelligent—32%. The Japanese tend to envision the West and Westerners in general as individualistic, with the Americans the most extreme example. But the British are not that far removed. One could assume that the Germans and French, for example, would register nearly the same as the British according to the image of indigenous cultural elements of Western people held by the Japanese teenagers.

The strong positive response (4 + 5) in the intelligent trait (62%) is surely indicative of respect toward the British partly in terms of admiration for not only Oxford and Cambridge Universities, but the most famous British Public Schools such as Eton as well. To many Japanese, these distinguished institutions personify British education, even though a very tiny percentage of British students attend such institutions, partly because they know so little about the rest of the system. Very little criticism of the British education system, which is widespread within Britain, reaches a Japanese audience. In contrast the most pungent American criticisms of American education are carried in the Japanese press, particularly coverage of school violence, literacy standards, and the low scores on comparative international tests, which are often contrasted with the high scores of Japanese students. Consequently nearly twice as many Japanese respondents (4 + 5: 62%) believe the British are highly intelligent people in comparison to their much lower perception of the Americans (26%) (see Table 21).

The lowest result in the most positive category of 5, taken from Table 20, falls tellingly in the trait of highly industrious, in which only 6.3% of the Japanese perceive the British as industrious people. The term "British disease," implying a complacent work force susceptible to downing tools at the least provocation, has made the rounds in Japan. The image of the British as hardworking people attached to the concept of *kimben* (industriousness) is not a close one. Still the negative categories of 1 and 2, not very industrious, drew only 13.2% in contrast to the comparable figure of 36.8% describing the Americans as being not very industrious. From this perspective, the Japanese perceive the British as more industrious than Americans. Both the British and Americans, however, fall far behind the positive image the Japanese have of their own people as industrious, accordingly (see Table 22).

Our final set of tables in this series presents the British perception of the Japanese and Americans. In this instance we are now able to compare how two Western peoples sharing much in common historically perceive the Japanese, and how they perceive each other. Again, as we know, Japan historically has experienced closer contacts with America than with

Table 21
Japanese student perception of intelligence

	Not very				Highly	
	1	2	3	4	5	(4 + 5)
British	2.8%	4.1%	27.9%	40.4%	21.6%	(62.0%)
Americans	6.9	14.2	50.2	21.7	4.3	(26.0)

Source: Excerpted from Tables 16 and 20.

Table 22
Japanese student perception of industriousness

	Not very				Highly	
	1	2	3	4	5	(4 + 5)
British	4.5%	8.7%	46.5%	30.2%	6.3%	(36.5%)
Americans	10.5	26.3	43.7	13.1	2.6	(15.7)
Japanese	0.9	2.4	8.1	24.2	62.7	(86.9)

Source: Excerpted from Tables 9, 16, and 20.

Britain. Nevertheless the Anglo-Japanese relationship is the second most important bilateral contact for the Japanese with the West and their major avenue into the new European Economic Community. The Anglo-American relationship, on the other hand, has formed the very foundation of the entire Western alliance in the modern period.

The major trait of the Japanese from this table as perceived by the outstanding British students is highly industrious (category 5 only), chosen by an impressive majority of 71.5% (see Table 23). This is in marked contrast to the 6.3% of the Japanese who conversely think the British are highly industrious people. On the other hand it corresponds very closely to the American image of the Japanese, with 69.1% describing them as highly industrious. In general, the image of the Japanese by Westerners is primarily affiliated with the concept of industriousness, whereas the prominent image of the two Western societies by the Japanese is one of individualism.

The concept of industriousness also attracts interest when the British image of the Japanese as industrious is compared in Table 24 with that of their image of British and American industriousness, the latter included in Table 27, which is presented later. The rank order not only places the British at the bottom, it also reveals a fairly wide gap between the Japanese at the top and the Americans in the runner-up position.

The next highest percentage in category 5, from Table 23 above, falls in the traits of loyalty (55.2%) and politeness (46.1%). In the Western tradition, loyalty and politeness, along with industriousness, are considered as fairly positive characteristics. In other words, the strongest images attributed to the Japanese by the British fall within traits thought to be exemplary. The most negative image of the Japanese comes within the area of individualism. One in four (25.5%) believe the Japanese are not very individualistic. This corresponds with the American image of the Japanese in terms of individualism (see Table 25). In fact, the responses of the Americans and British are so similar, they must be seen together in

Table 23
British student perception of the Japanese

	Not very				Highly
	1	2	3	4	5
Creative	6.6%	7.8%	22.0%	31.4%	30.7%
Loyal	3.0	3.9	12.6	23.8	55.2
Emotional	15.0	23.7	28.9	18.2	12.3
Materialistic	3.6	11.4	27.3	24.7	26.1
Individualistic	25.5	32.0	21.7	12.3	6.5
Industrious	1.5	0.8	4.9	19.8	71.5
Generous	9.1	17.3	45.7	19.2	6.4
Trustworthy	10.1	12.9	33.0	29.1	12.6
Polite	3.7	3.6	15.2	30.0	46.1
Forgiving	13.6	22.0	45.7	12.9	5.0
Aggressive	6.7	17.2	29.0	26.6	17.8
Intelligent	3.5	2.0	16.8	43.0	33.1

Table 24
British student perception of industriousness

	Not very				Highly
	1	2	3	4	5
Americans	4.0%	7.9%	37.4%	39.3%	9.5%
British	5.2	18.9	42.0	25.5	6.8
Japanese	1.5	0.8	4.9	19.8	71.5

Source: Excerpted from Tables 8, 23, and 27.

Table 25
**American and British student perception of the Japanese
as individualistic**

	Not very				Highly
	1	2	3	4	5
By Americans	22.7%	30.4%	22.0%	10.2%	7.3%
By British	25.5	32.0	21.7	12.3	6.5

Source: Excerpted from Tables 10 and 23.

Table 26
British student perception of creativity

	Not very			Highly		
	1	2	3	4	5	(4 + 5)
Americans	9.2%	18.0%	34.0%	28.1%	9.2%	(37.3%)
British	2.3	13.6	34.3	29.9	18.7	(48.6)
Japanese	6.6	7.8	22.0	31.4	30.7	(62.1)

Source: Excerpted from Tables 8, 23, and 27.

order to fully appreciate how common the Western perception of the Japanese people is.

Surely one of the most significant indications of British attitudes toward the Japanese, signaling important reactions concerning Japanese products and the increase in Japanese plants in the United Kingdom, concerns their image of the Japanese in terms of creativity. The response as seen in Table 26 is quite positive. But that image should be placed in the context of their image of creativity among their own people and that of the Americans, presented in Table 27, who have so often been considered by peoples around the world as very creative. Contemporary British youth have a different perspective.

The last table completes the cycle. The image one Western people has of another enables us to make the contrast between West and West, and East and West.

There are no extreme results that stand out in Table 27. The strongest trait falls in highly materialistic, with 56.5% choosing it. The next, somewhat surprisingly, comes in highly emotional (40.1) and reinforces the Japanese image of Americans on this character aspect. Even highly aggressive, a trait we have been led to believe that Europeans consider

Table 27
British student perception of Americans

| | Not very | | | | Highly |
	1	2	3	4	5
Creative	9.2%	18.0%	34.0%	28.1%	9.2%
Loyal	6.4	14.9	32.4	26.3	18.7
Emotional	2.7	5.1	20.1	30.1	40.1
Materialistic	2.5	3.4	15.6	20.1	56.5
Individualistic	7.1	13.0	28.0	27.2	22.6
Industrious	4.0	7.9	37.4	39.3	9.5
Generous	5.6	13.0	30.9	35.7	13.3
Trustworthy	14.8	19.9	40.6	18.5	4.2
Polite	17.4	25.4	29.9	17.5	8.2
Forgiving	11.2	22.9	40.7	19.0	3.9
Aggressive	2.7	5.3	20.7	37.7	31.8
Intelligent	14.3	15.2	34.7	28.2	6.0

characteristically American, only drew 31.8% as the next most vivid image. This is a tempered image of the Americans similar to the moderate image the Americans have of the British.

Between two nations that have maintained the closest relations in the past, the most negative trait of not very trustworthy held by 14.8% of the future leaders of Britain could be considered as somewhat noteworthy. Only 4.2% claimed the Americans are highly trustworthy, representing the lowest result in this category. Again, for two nations with intimate political and strategic interests, this figure is not comforting to anyone concerned with their future relationships.

The low figures of 6% for highly intelligent and 9.5% for highly industrious are also not strong indications of a positive attitude toward Americans by the British. The Americans, in comparison, characterized the British as highly intelligent by only 14.3% and highly industrious by only 9.5%. Both attributed a much more positive response on both traits to the

Table 28
British student perception of intelligence

| | Not very | | | | Highly | |
	1	2	3	4	5	(4 + 5)
British	3.0%	5.5%	32.2%	38.4%	19.0%	(57.4%)
Americans	14.3	15.2	34.7	28.2	6.0	(34.2)
Japanese	3.5	2.0	16.8	43.0	33.1	(76.1)

Source: Excerpted from Tables 8, 23, and 27.

Japanese than they did to each other. In other words both the Americans and the British have a more positive image of the Japanese, their common foe in the middle of this century, than they do of each other, not only in terms of industriousness but also creativity, previously described, and intelligence (see Table 28).

Several additional questions were included to confirm and/or reinforce the profiles drawn from the various evaluations presented above. The final one in this series was a simple straightforward assessment of the impressions each group of our outstanding students has toward the others. The focus, however, was on the Western student attitude toward the Japanese, and vice versa.

An impressive majority of 70% of the American students currently enrolled in the most outstanding secondary schools in the United States, receiving in effect the best education America has to offer, believe the Japanese are the best educated people among the three choices (see Question 28). In contrast, only 16% believe that the Americans are the best educated. Clearly the American students do not have a very positive image of the educational standards of their own people, as we have seen previously. This contrasts with nearly half of both the British (48.7%) and Japanese (46.7%) students who think their own people are the best educated among the three.

Another interesting result is found in the 26.4% of the Japanese

Question 28
Which people are the best educated?

	Americans	British	Japanese
The American people?	16.3%	6.8%	26.4%
The British people?	8.6	48.7	21.9
The Japanese people?	70.4	41.3	46.7

students who describe Americans as the best educated, a figure ten points higher than the number of Americans themselves who think that the Americans are the best-educated people. The opposite result is seen in the figure of 70.4% of Americans who believe the Japanese are the best educated in comparison to the 46.7% of the Japanese who think the Japanese people qualify for that distinction. The British (6.8%) place the Americans in a distant third position. Likewise the Americans (8.6%) relegate the British to the bottom of the educational ladder.

The comparative evaluation of the educational standards of the three peoples is an integral function of their general respect for one another (see Question 29). Although the question on respect was designed only as an East-West question, the attitudes toward educational standards closely relate to the overall respect one people have for another. With an extremely high category of great respect among the possible answers, the respondents must hold a very strong opinion in order to choose such a positive catgory. Consequently the 40% of American students who chose the category "I have great respect for the Japanese people" is a reflection of the 70% who chose the Japanese people as the best educated among the three.

Question 29
What impression do you (American and British students)
have of the Japanese? What impression do you (Japanese students)
have of the British and Americans?

```
              - American and British students -

                                  Americans   British

Great respect                       40.4%      23.6%

Some respect                        49.8       59.8

Little respect                       4.6        9.1

No respect                           1.9        6.3


                  - Japanese students -

                                  British    Americans

Great respect                       7.8%       5.5%

Some respect                       53.3       45.7

Little respect                     26.7       31.8

No respect                         11.1       15.9
```

On the other hand the 37 % of the Japanese who have little or no re-spect for the American people may be considered as surprisingly high. There are several explanations for this negative response. First of all, many Japanese are aware of the problems of illiteracy in America. They often read in the press and view on TV coverage emanating from the U.S. government itself depicting the unfortunate situation of millions of American adults who cannot read. American reports carried in the Japa-nese media usually refer to a figure of 23 million American adults who are functionally illiterate, a statistic that staggers the imagination of the Japa-nese public in a nation that regards itself as the most literate nation in the world. The Japanese know, too, that to achieve that literacy level requires an enormous effort by them, which the Americans fail to exert to accom-plish a similar standard.

Most Japanese, including our students, are also aware to some degree of the differences in educational standards between elementary and second-ary schools in America and Japan. The continuing large-scale immigra-tion of non-English-speaking foreigners, many from destitute countries in Latin America and Southeast Asia, is another well-known fact about con-temporary American society that influences Japanese student attitudes toward Americans in general. All in all it is not a flattering image.

There is a technical element in the translation of the word "respect" into Japanese that deserves noting. In the context of this question, it was difficult to arrive at a consensus among several Japanese educators who approved the Japanese version of the questionnaire on the appropriate translation of the English word "respect." After much deliberation the word *sonkei* was finally agreed upon as coming the closest to respect, although it was generally agreed that this carried just a bit more positive attitude toward another person than the English concept of respect. Still, the category of *zenzen sonkei shinai* (no respect) is decidedly negative, although the next category above it, *sonna ni sonkei wa shite inai*, should not be considered quite as negative as the English phrase "little respect," which can have a decidedly negative connotation. Nevertheless the Japanese translation is not positive either.

In summarizing the results of this series of questions, perhaps the most poignant way to characterize them would be under the heading of "changing perceptions." We do not have similar studies from the past with which to compare, but rather commonly accepted perceptions of one nation by another to use as our basis for comparison. Employing that as our measure, the images all three peoples have of each other are, among this group of highly selected outstanding students, currently undergoing significant changes.

Surely one of the major factors underlying the changing perceptions seen above can be attributed to the new role of Japan in the modern world. Where once the British and Americans were characterized as the most industrious people in the world, the Japanese have overwhelmingly replaced them in a category that all three people most admire. In the area of creativity, through modern history the Japanese have been described in both the East and the West as imitators of things created in the West. This generation of Western students views the Japanese as creative people themselves. And so it goes throughout the study. The Japanese people are perceived in very positive terms in most traits that are admired by Western peoples. In many instances the degree of positiveness surpasses the image our two groups of Western students have not only of themselves but of each other.

Of equal if not greater significance is evidence from the statistics that shows the future leaders of Japan perceive the Japanese people in a new image, generally quite positive, similar to that perceived by the Western students. Even though they cannot yet imagine Japan as a nation rivaling major Western countries as a world leader, their image of the Japanese people stands out as positive. On the other hand, the Japanese perception of our two Western peoples who have played such a dominant role in world events, and in recent Japanese history, is perhaps more critical today than at any time in the modern period. The exception, of course, is the wartime period when Japan fought against both America and Britain. An assumption could follow that the future leaders of Japan envision their nation ready to assume a position of world leadershp commensurate with their new status as an economic superpower. This critical issue will be considered in the final chapter after various other perceptions are analyzed, most notably about the future.

5

TRADE FRICTION

Made in Japan

Trade imbalances between Japan and the United States, and to a lesser degree between Japan and Britain, have become the primary source of contention in otherwise fairly amicable bilateral relationships. Japan has been recording grossly one-sided balance of payment surpluses with the United States annually for nearly a decade. Although not of the same proportions, a similar trend has characterized trade patterns between Japan and Britain. Even Japanese government and industrial leaders have become alarmed over the annual trade figures, which undermine diplomatic relations between close allies. The problem, although multifaceted, stems to a considerable extent from the irresistible attractiveness of Japanese products to consumers on the domestic markets of the United States, Britain, and Japan itself. Herculean efforts have been undertaken by all sides as policy objectives to stem the tidal wave of Japanese exports and increase imports into Japan. Nevertheless the imbalance continues.

The influence of Japan's immensely favorable trade balance with the United States extends far beyond export-import figures. During the past decade of annual imbalances, Japan has accumulated vast sums of foreign currency, mostly dollars, that have been recycled into the international channels of finance and investment. The two primary vehicles employed by the nation's bankers and corporate leaders as long-term investment policies have been U.S. Treasury offerings and American real estate. In its own unique manner, each channel has caused considerable anxiety and reaction within the American financial and political communities, as well as with the American public at large.

Because of the magnitude of Japanese investments in U.S. Treasury bonds, the American government has come to rely on them in order to finance the continuing national budget deficits. One of the most critical indicators of the stability of the American financial system relates directly to the response by Japanese investors to the scheduled auctions of U.S. Treasury bonds, notes, and bills. In other words, American policy makers find themselves in the classic catch-22 dilemma. If their concerted effort to reduce the trade imbalance with Japan succeeds, they restrict Japan's ability to buy U.S. Treasury offerings, which undergirds the American national budget. If, on the other hand, the trading patterns are not brought into balance, American competitive power is further reduced as Japan expands its influence into global markets once dominated by American firms or captures markets for new products. Both trends are already well under way.

The second result of Japan's huge trade surpluses, increased investments in American real estate, receives much more attention in America than the massive Japanese purchases of U.S. Treasury offerings. Although Japanese ownership of American bonds may be of greater national consequence in the long run than their ownership of U.S. real estate, few Americans outside the financial community are aware of the extent to which Japanese funds indirectly finance the national deficit. Nevertheless the high visibility of Japanese real estate transactions, from controlling interest in Rockefeller Center in the east to Columbia Pictures in the west, has sparked widespread concern that the Japanese are "buying up America." Lawmakers at various levels periodically introduce legislation to restrict or control foreign investments in American property, invariably aimed at Japanese investors. And yet about half of all U.S. state governments maintain representative offices in Japan fervently searching out potential Japanese investors to their states. Ironically, at a time when criticism of Japanese real estate investments in America is proliferating, a new industry has emerged in America of specialists, including government bureaus, peddling American real estate to the Japanese.

American trade negotiators have taken a new approach to the perennial problem of trade imbalances with Japan for the 1990s. Rather than concentrating on restricting Japanese imports to America through quotas, or increasing Japanese plants producing Japanese products made in America, a policy decision in the opposite direction was made. The American negotiators are now not only demanding that Japan reduce all barriers to American imports, but enormous pressure is being applied on Japan to restructure its traditional ways of conducting domestic affairs. These demands, which are couched in very strong, even threatening language, include, for example, laws that would encourage large retail stores such as supermarkets replacing the traditional small Japanese shopkeeper. This new policy places the American negotiators directly into domestic matters of Japanese custom and social traditions fashioned over the centuries that go far beyond the marketplace.

Many knowledgeable financial critics in Japan and elsewhere speculate that even if most of the American demands were met by the Japanese side, the trade imbalances might be lowered in the near future, but not by much. The ultimate issue still depends on the competitive ability of manufacturers on both sides to attract the consumer, not only in Japan, America, and Britain, but throughout the global market, to buy their products. Because trade friction looms as the paramount source of contention in the respective bilateral relationships, a series of pertinent but simple questions was posed to all 3,000 students concerning products and trading practices.

Western-style capitalism, the so-called market system, represents the economic common denominator among Japan, America, and Britain. The well-being of their people depends to a great extent on the competitiveness of their products at the global marketplace. The determinant of success in this vital contest rests very much on the price and quality of the end product. The nation that can build an image of its products as reasonably priced and of dependable quality forges ahead of the pack, placing its people in an advantageous position to quicken the pace and extend the lead into new industries. In an era of high technology, the nation that sells its products most successfully is positioned to become the most technologically advanced nation in the world.

The results of this poll demonstrate convincingly that the Japanese have achieved in all three countries an impressive lead in the positive perception of their products, an essential ingredient in marketing their goods (see Question 30). A strong majority of American and British youth believe that Japanese products are superior to American and British products. A significant majority, over 80% in the case of the British respondents, also believe that Japanese products are less expensive than American and British products. The image of Japanese products in terms of quality and pricing underlies to a considerable extent the continuing trade imbalances between Japan and her two major Western trading competitors.

Of great importance in this poll is the attitude of the Japanese toward their own products. It should be recalled that the Japanese people tend look to America for new trends in fashion, music, food, politics, and a myriad of other areas both material and otherwise. American trends in virtually every sector have had a major influence on Japanese society since the end of the war. It would not, therefore, be inconceivable to expect that the Japanese would also look to America in product design and manufacturing, that American products would be the model for Japanese products, and that, for example, an American car would be preferred over a Japanese car as are designer jeans.

Question 30
How do you feel about Japanese products?

- American and British Students -

Many Japanese products are superior to our products.

	Agree	Disagree	No opinion
Americans	73.5%	14.4%	16.5%
British	60.6	25.6	13.6

- Japanese Students -

Many Japanese products are superior to:

American products	76.5%	4.2%	17.1%
British products	73.4	4.2	19.2

- American and British Students -

In general, Japanese products

are less expensive than our products.

Americans	64.4%	22.6%	11.3%
British	80.8	9.9	9.2

- Japanese Students -

In general, Japanese products

are less expensive than:

American products	34.4%	34.4%	28.6%
British products	37.3	28.0	32.3

Our poll proves this not to be the case. Three out of four Japanese students agree with a majority of their Western peers vis-à-vis the superior quality of Japanese products. Their common perception of Japanese products unites them as little else does. It sets the framework for the trade imbalances firmly in place. American and British youth prefer Japanese products over their own in such large numbers that domestically produced goods too often cannot effectively compete in their home markets, and decidedly so on the Japanese domestic market. In this sense, the trade imbalances are made in Japan.

One of the major demands made by both the American and British governments, in their frustrated attempts to rectify the trade imbalances with Japan, has taken the form of promoting Japanese imports from their respective countries. Our statistics clarify the challenges confronting this policy in the manufacturing sector. Excluding foodstuffs, where Japan cannot possibly compete due to its greatly restricted land size supporting a large population, Japanese youth overwhelmingly prefer Japanese products over British and American imports. That attitude renders it extremely difficult for American and British goods to compete with Japanese products in Japan. The only major difference in the results above are that far fewer Japanese believe their products sold in Japan are less expensive than imports, stemming in part from the general feeling among Japanese that virtually everything in Japan is more expensive than elsewhere. In most instances that conclusion is correct.

The interviews also revealed an underlying problem that seldom surfaces during trade negotiations but plays perhaps a significant role in distorting the annual trade figures. Japanese manufacturers give major attention to after-purchase care. This condition was reflected when our Japanese students mentioned that one of the reasons they are reluctant to buy expensive American products is the lack of service facilities in Japan when repairs and parts are needed. Both American and British students did not find this an inhibiting problem when contemplating the purchase of Japanese products in their countries. A service network for Japanese products was available in both America and Britain extending even fairly far into the rural areas.

These various factors come into play in the formation of an image of a nation's products, and the people who produce them, that shows up in this study. To confirm the response to the above questions, all students were asked to compare products from all three countries in the following straightforward question (see Question 31).

The confirmation appears. In an unmistakable comparison of American, British, and Japanese products, a majority of all of our future leaders chose Japanese products as superior. What is of similar import is that American products score so low. In simple figures, approximately 300 students out of the 3,000 who participated in this study believe that American products are the best among the three. Even British students (35.8%) have a more positive impression of British products than Ameri-

Question 31
In general, which produce the best and most reliable products?

	Americans	British	Japanese
American companies	21.3%	5.5%	2.4%
British companies	4.8	35.8	3.3
Japanese companies	69.7	56.2	91.8

can students (21.3%) of American products. From this perspective, made in America, if made by American companies, that is, no longer remains a persuasive selling point. In fact it could possibly be somewhat detrimental for marketing purposes within the United States itself. The same may be true for American products in Japan and England as well.

With only 5.5% of the British and 2.4% of the Japanese recognizing American products as superior among the three, the uphill battle for American industry to compete with Japanese products in foreign markets, as well as in their own, is made abundantly clear. In other words both the Japanese and British prefer Japanese over American products. But British industry faces a similar problem since only 3.3% of the Japanese and 4.8% of the Americans consider British products as the best of the three. In every market and among all three groups of students, the image of Japanese products as superior stands out.

The stark reality and enormous significance of the response to this simple question of which country produces the best products must not be underestimated by policy makers in America and Britain. The group of students who responded with this most positive image of Japanese products are representative of future opinion makers themselves. They will someday hold positions of influence in virtually every sector of the society in all three countries. Having leaders who perceive Japanese products with such unanimity making decisons and influencing policies in the three nations and throughout the society is a factor of major consequence in the overall relations between these countries.

Several other factors are claimed by both the American and British governments, as well as many of their businessmen, as responsible for the trade imbalances between Japan and her Western competitors. The most prominent one is included in this survey (see Question 32). The Japanese also argue that other issues affect the competitive edge their products have attained over American and British goods. One of their most prominent charges was also posed to all three groups of outstanding students to gauge their reaction.

In addition to the very positive price-and-quality image of Japanese

Question 32
Do you think Japan has unfair trading practices that keep
American and British products out of Japanese markets?

	Yes	No	No opinion
Americans	42.0%	21.0%	34.6%
British	52.1	14.3	33.5
Japanese	28.6	36.5	32.6

products among all three groups, the negative aspect of unfair trading practices by the Japanese is also perceived as a factor in the overall equation among a substantial segment of the respondents. Even 28.6% of the Japanese students believe their own country is guilty of what many Western critics charge as playing the trading game on an uneven track. Only 36.5% of the Japanese defend their country against this general criticism from many countries endeavoring to expand their exports into the potentially lucrative but difficult to penetrate Japanese domestic market. Perhaps no other criticism of Japanese trading practices strikes the American public so emotionally as the perception that the Japanese pursue unfair trading practices giving them an advantage at the marketplace.

Caution is advised here as well. There are respected analysts who claim that even if all Japanese trading practices charged by the American and British governments and traders as unfair were abolished, trade imbalances would be reduced only marginally as a result. Japanese specialists insist that almost all of the so-called unfair practices have already been eliminated or are well on their way out. Regardless of the validity of the respective positions, the most fundamental condition remains. Consumers in all three countries prefer Japanese products over their own on the most powerful factors of price and reliability.

Swinging back to a positive image of Japanese trading practices claimed by the Japanese side, there is widespread agreement among the three nationalities on the question of sales effort (see Question 33). Only about 15% of each group believe that the Japanese do not work harder than their foreign counterparts in marketing goods abroad. Those who contend that the unfair trading practices by the Japanese have been eliminated argue that Western businessmen simply refuse to allot the funds and effort to break into the Japanese markets, as the Japanese sacrificed to penetrate the American and British markets. The general image of the hardworking Japanese cited in the previous chapter, both in Japan and abroad, strengthens this positive image of the Japanese in the highly competitive arena of international trade. It is a picture of the aggressive Japa-

Question 33
Do you think the Japanese work harder to sell Japanese products
in America and Britain than do the American and British in trying
to sell their products in Japan?

	Yes	No	No opinion
American	57.9%	16.6%	23.6%
British	65.0	15.0	19.8
Japanese	60.0	12.3	25.3

nese businessman that is envisioned by the Westerner when contemplating trading patterns with Japan.

In this writer's weekly seminar of Japanese businessmen, the argument that American businessmen are not prepared to sustain the trials and tribulations required to penetrate foreign markets is supported by what could be appropriately described as war stories from the business world. One member, the president of a medium-size Japanese firm, had acquired an ailing American company in a bid to enter the American market. During the first two years of operation, annual losses running into the millions of dollars were sustained, significantly eroding the overall financial picture of the parent company when the losses from the American subsidiary were factored into the annual financial report presented to the stockholders meeting. When asked how long he was prepared to endure such losses, he explained that his company hoped to turn the American company around in about five more years or so. He added that his small subsidiary firm in China had been taking losses for nearly ten years, and that he was prepared to endure for another ten years to make a profit from that investment in a potentially huge future consumer market. With a sparkle in his eye, he wondered whether his American competitors were prepared to make similar long-term sacrifices for foreign market shares.

In reaction to the economic impact of prolonged imbalances of trade between Japan and America, and Japan and Britain, some representatives of sectors suffering from Japan's superior position have demanded far more stringent action against the Japanese. More specifically, various politicians in both countries have, on occasion, urged retaliatory measures against the Japanese, such as import restrictions. There are not a few people in both America and Britain who support this drastic unilateral measure. The term "Japan bashing" was coined to describe this type of harsh reaction. The consequence of such measures was included in the following question appropriately posed to all three groups (see Question 34).

An ambivalent attitude toward trade restrictions appears as the students in both England and the United States not only react in the same manner, but they also split evenly on the issue. The reason that a majority did not support restrictive measures as advocated by critics in both countries is, in part, because of the realization that such action would result in higher prices for the Japanese products upon which so many of this youthful generation in the survey have become dependent. On the other side, only 50% of the Japanese disagree with the idea of foreign governments restricting Japanese imports. This moderation was partially based on the belief by Japanese students that the Japanese government resorts to unfair trading practices, polled in a previous question, in which only 36.5% openly disagreed with that criticism.

In both America and Britain, the strategy by the Japanese to recycle part of the annual trade imbalances by increased investments in manufac-

Question 34
How do you feel about restricting Japanese imports?

- American and British Students -

Our government should restrict Japanese imports

even though it would make them more expensive.

	Agree	Disagree	No opinion
Americans	39.3%	39.0%	19.2%
British	40.8	41.3	17.0

- Japanese Students -

Japanese imports should be restricted

even though it would make them more expensive:

	Agree	Disagree	No opinion
By the Americans	11.7%	50.8%	34.9%
By the British	10.5	49.1	37.9

turing facilities in their respective countries has been welcomed. Many Japanese companies have responded by building more plants to produce their goods in America and Britain, using local employees both on the line and in management. The Japanese automobile industry has become one of the major sectors in this overseas expansion of manufacturing capabilities. Our future leaders were asked to react to this trend directly, and in a very personal way (see Question 35).

Although both American and British governments encourage Japanese investments in their countries, and foreign businessmen and local government leaders, especially American state and local representatives, make a concerted effort to attract investments into their area, a major note of caution is evident from this survey. Only 13.6% of the American students approve of this effort in their country. The backlash toward Japanese investments in America has clearly penetrated this group of future American leaders. A majority oppose a further increase. The concept of selling out America to the Japanese cannot be dismissed as misguided, although British and even Dutch investments in America rival Japanese portfolios. Nevertheless the Japanese are being singled out for criticism. The desire for Japanese investment funds in America to stimulate local and regional economies must be tempered by the strong opposition that is reflected in this study.

The follow-up personal interviews exposed a depth of antagonism toward further Japanese investments overseas worth noting. A twinge of

Question 35
How do you feel about companies expanding abroad?

- American and British Students -

There should be more Japanese companies

establishing offices and factories in our country.

	Agree	Disagree	No opinion
Americans	13.6%	58.6%	25.7%
British	31.2	44.4	23.9

- Japanese Students -

There should be more Japanese companies

establishing offices and factories:

	Agree	Disagree	No opinion
In America	39.0%	27.6%	30.8%
In Britain	38.6	26.8	31.9

- Japanese Students -

There should be more foreign companies

establishing offices and factories in Japan:

	Agree	Disagree	No opinion
By American companies	36.1%	25.9%	35.4%
By British companies	35.2	25.7	36.0

ambivalence was detected as well. Among our Western students, there runs a strong feeling of admiration for the Japanese people and their accomplishments as a nation, evidenced throughout this study. Simultaneously a certain sense of resentment toward the Japanese is expressed that they have been able to achieve those accomplishments, as one student described it, "partly at our expense." Media coverage of Japanese investments in America ignites latent resentment, motivated in part by what is perceived as Japan's unfair trading practices. And yet admiration for the diligent and industrious Japanese people cannot be dismissed lightly. Our American students in particular represent what can be considered as a widespread ambivalent attitude toward the Japanese by the American public at large, reignited with each announcement of seemingly endless acquisitions of American property by Japanese investors.

Among British students, one in three support their government's very active campaign to attract more Japanese investments in Britain. In the first chapter, the British ambassador to Japan was quoted in a university lecture as saying that "there are virtually no problems at all regarding Japanese investments in the United Kingdom." However, 44.4% disagree with that policy, indicating that the British government should be as cautious as American leaders about promoting a campaign to encourage local Japanese investments. Economically it may be desirable, but emotionally and politically it should be pursued with great caution.

On the Japanese side, about 40% approve of further investments abroad. At the end of the 1980s and the beginning of the 1990s when this survey was conducted, it was fashionable to think internationally and promote the cause of internationalism. This was noteworthy not only by commercial investments abroad. Japanese educational institutions were also establishing campuses in America and Britain to accommodate Japanese students for study abroad. To our Japanese participants, it is all part of the internationalization of Japan.

On the other hand only about one in three approve of more foreign investments in Japan. In a small country like Japan supporting a population half that of America on a livable area about 15% the size of the state of Montana, there is literally very little land available for development. The participants in this study are well aware of the consequence of Japan's precarious geographical restrictions: the exorbitant cost of real estate. Although the concept of foreign investments in itself was not the main concern, the reality of the enormous investments required starting from scratch with the purchase of facilities and plants greatly restricts the opportunities for foreign investors, as it does for the Japanese as well, in the minds of our students. The specter of further pressure for space by foreigners is not a welcomed prospect, revealing the mentality of a people long accustomed to perceiving their country as small.

The prospect of working for a Japanese company by our American and British students divides them internally rather evenly (see Question 36). They are generally aware of the growing number of Japanese factories in their respective countries, but as students are less knowledgeable about labor relations between the local work force and their Japanese managers. Those who have some knowledge about labor relations in Japanese-owned factories from the various reports about conditions view the prospect of working in them positively. In some contrast, the Japanese take a more favorable attitude toward working for a foreign company in Japan, particularly American. The very fact that IBM Japan has cultivated an enviable reputation among the top ten companies in the nation attracting one of the highest number of applicants from Japan's universities strengthens the positive attitude toward working for a foreign company in Japan.

Question 36
How do you feel about working for a foreign company?

- American and British Students -

I would not mind working for a Japanese company in our

country under the supervision of a Japanese manager.

	Agree	Disagree	No opinion
Americans	39.6%	36.4%	22.3%
British	46.6	35.3	17.6

- Japanese Students -

I would not mind working for an American or British company

in Japan under an American or British manager.

	Agree	Disagree	No opinion
An American company	58.3%	25.1%	14.6%
A British company	46.6	35.3	17.6

It would appear that Japanese companies planning to build more factories or expand existing facilities in America or Britain can do so with a certain degree of confidence concerning the local work force. Apparently there will be sufficient numbers of willing employees to meet their demands. The Japanese may be racially and socially different from those predominant in our two Western countries, but these factors need not stand in the way of successful overseas investments in manufacturing facilities by Japanese companies.

Product recognition and identification are critical factors in the highly competitive business world. The answers to Question 37 identify one more strand of evidence demonstrating how thoroughly Japanese products have penetrated the psyche of Western youth. More than eight out of ten American and British youth recognize the name of a Japanese car. This presumably includes a number of them who are not particularly interested in cars but are still familiar with the Japanese name. The advertising campaigns as well as the attractiveness and reliability of Japanese products, as revealed in a previous question, have obviously been most effective in indelibly stamping the made-in-Japan logo in the minds of American and British youth.

On the other hand, less than half of our outstanding Japanese youth can identify one of the most common American cars on the market and one identified with the mass market of automobiles in America. Likewise less than half could identify one of the most famous British cars on the inter-

Question 37
Student recognition of foreign products

- American and British Students -

Which is a Japanese car?

	Volvo	Toyota	Hyundai	Mercedes
Americans	0.9%	84.9%	11.7%	0.2%
British	0.4	92.4	6.3	0.2

- Japanese Students -

Which is an American or British car?

	Volvo	Mercedes	Chevrolet	Jaguar
An American car?	11.2%	10.6%	41.6%	28.4%
A British car?	16.1	8.0	22.7	44.1

national market. Clearly foreign firms have not been able to penetrate the Japanese psyche with their product names to any comparable degree with the Japanese. This is reflected in a previous question in which about 60% of the Western students agree that the Japanese work harder to sell their products in the American and British markets.

These various statistics concerning attitudes toward American, British, and Japanese products reveal a consistent pattern. The future leaders of our three countries overwhelmingly favor Japanese products. Student interviews in the three countries reinforce this conclusion. When given the hypothetical situation where the student had the choice of purchasing a British brand, American brand, or Japanese brand television set, automobile, or any other product of equal price and appearance, which would they purchase? The vast majority would choose the Japanese brand. When asked why, the ultimate consumer reaction was simply that "It's a good product."

The American government and commercial and industrial leaders have exerted an enormous effort during the two years of this survey to reduce the huge trade imbalances with Japan that have been running around $50 billion a year in Japan's favor. Their strategy has been to attack the problem from two major positions. The first, mentioned previously, is to sharply increase the amount of American exports to Japan, primarily in the form of foodstuffs and high technology, such as satellites. Symbolic of the negotiations has been the U.S. demand for access to Japanese markets for American-grown rice, a staple with deep cultural as well as political significance to the Japanese people.

The second position is to encourage Japanese firms to make capital investments in America in the form of manufacturing facilities to produce Japanese products in America by American workers. This would theoretically reduce the trade imbalances while simultaneously expanding employment opportunities for the American work force. It could also stimulate local economies in a multiplicity of ways with an influx of foreign capital otherwise unavailable in local areas. The process is well under way.

Japanese-American trade talks during this particular study have become the focus of polemical negotiations as the American position hardened. Harsh criticisms of Japan were expressed not only by American politicians whose constituencies are affected by the trade imbalances, such as Michigan, the center of the American automobile industry. They were also issued by the American trade negotiators themselves as the so-called trade friction intensified

Out of frustration over the lack of substantive reductions in the trade imbalances, the Americans ultimately presented a series of demands to the Japanese government during the oddly named Structural Impediments Initiative negotiations. At the heart of the American position were such domestically oriented demands as that Japan revise its laws regarding the restrictions on large-scale stores, already referred to; strict enforcement of its antimonopoly regulations; and increased expenditures on the social infrastructure of the country such as roads, bridges, and sewers. The nature of the American demands, which appeared to the Japanese as somewhat irrelevant to the basic issues of international trade, were received with some puzzlement. They were further complicated by the insistence of the American negotiators that the Japanese government notify the American government of the precise future budgets for such items as highway construction. Many Japanese felt that the American negotiators were purposely ignoring the basic issues of quality and pricing of goods at the marketplace, where Japanese products, as revealed in this survey, exert a strong appeal to the customer.

In response to the demands from both the American and British governments and their local political and industrial leaders, Japanese firms have invested heavily in building plants in both the United States and Britain. One company alone, Nissan Motors, has built huge plants in Tennessee and Newcastle that in themselves have attracted a host of other Japanese companies to the area. The effort to attract more and more Japanese firms to America and Britain continues at a hectic pace under appeals by the receiving governments. In spite of all of these efforts, the trade imbalances continue, as before, in Japan's favor.

To summarize the most important results from this portion of the study, then, our survey of the future leaders of America and Britain reveals an attitude that should not be taken lightly by the contemporary leaders of both countries. Nearly 60% of the American students and 45% of the British students disagree with the policy of establishing more Japanese factories in their countries. On the contrary, only 13.6% of the Americans supported the idea. Among the British, a higher percentage of 31.2% approved it.

During the student interviews, as described above, deep concern was expressed by both British and, particularly, American students over an increase in Japanese investments in their respective countries. Reflecting the survey data, British students were somewhat more responsive to Japanese investments than the Americans. This was especially noticeable with students from the north of Britain where Japanese plants have made a very positive impact on the economy of a once-depressed area. Those students welcomed more Japanese factories.

There is without doubt great concern by the American students about more Japanese investments in the United States. Economically the policy may be considered vital by American trade negotiators in redirecting the distorted trading patterns. Politically and diplomatically, however, the survey of attitudes of future American leaders reveals widespread opposition. Japanese leaders should be as concerned over these negative attitudes as the Americans since the long-term relationship between two close postwar allies is at stake.

The American trade negotiators must also face the implications of the data from this survey concerning the highly favorable attitudes all three groups of students hold for Japanese products. Even though 42% of the American students and 52% of the British students believe that Japan has unfair trading practices that restrict imports for the Japanese domestic markets, there can be little prospect of a significant improvement in trade imbalances even if all so-called unfair trading practices are eliminated. American products will not attract Japanese consumers in sufficient quantities to bring about any significant shift in the trading patterns when they believe so strongly that Japanese products are superior.

An additional significant factor in the poor image of American products in comparison to Japanese products is that the Japanese are not the only ones who hold this opinion. American and British youth reinforce that attitude as well in a straightforward comparison of products according to the country of origin. British students not only prefer Japanese products over British goods, they also prefer Japanese products over American products on the British markets, such is the reputation of Japanese manufacturers. In market after market throughout so many areas of the world, Japanese products have been capturing increasing shares for their products over American goods. What is of such great concern to American industry is that the same trend is apparently under way within America itself.

The data from this survey demonstrate the depth of the problem both the British and the American governments and their industrial leaders face in their frustrating efforts to reduce the imbalances in trade with Japan. The problem is obviously greater for the Americans due to the sheer magnitude of the annual trade imbalance. It is not an exaggeration to predict that even if all the demands by the American trade negotiators for reciprocity, removal of structural impediments, and so on, were met by the Japanese, the trade imbalance between the two countries would remain distorted in favor of Japan. Until consumer confidence in American products, both abroad and at home, matches that of Japanese products, trading patterns will not balance out even though Japan has become dependent on American foodstuffs.

The issue takes on an even greater urgency in considering the results of this particular study. Our student participants are representative of the future leaders of America, Britain, and Japan. As recorded previously, substantive research shows that basic attitudes held by youth at this stage of maturity are carried into adulthood. The implications are clear. Unless Japanese product standards deteriorate over the years, which seems most unlikely, the future leaders who will be developing trade policy for America and Britain with Japan will be negotiating from an awkward position. While greatly appreciating the quality of Japanese products, they must endeavor to either restrict them as imports or undertake the monumental task of improving American and British products in an effort to render them competitive at the marketplace. Any approach other than the latter to overcome the underlying issue of superior quality of Japanese products, and a tireless effort by their salesmen to market them at home and abroad, will most likely meet with limited success.

6

PREDICTING THE FUTURE

The Japanese Century?

The turn of each century marks a milestone in the unfolding history of mankind. The year 2000 is particularly historical because it heralds the first full century of high technology in the modern world. Consequently many of our 3,000 outstanding secondary school students destined to become leaders of the next century will assume positions of responsibility for decision making under unprecedented circumstances. They truly represent the vanguard of leaders for a new era. The questions included in this chapter were designed to determine the perceptions of the twenty-first century by many of those who will become the leaders of it. They were, in effect, asked to predict the future as they envision it.

For students enrolled in outstanding schools in their respective countries, a generally positive attitude about their future could be anticipated (see Question 38). Still, particularly among the Western students, the

Question 38
How do you feel about your future?

	Americans	British	Japanese
Very positive	57.9%	42.9%	14.6%
Somewhat positive	36.2	48.3	62.9
Somewhat pessimistic	4.1	7.1	17.1
Very pessimisic	0.7	1.3	4.6

highly optimistic attitude they hold for their future is impressive, and encouraging as well. They face the future with considerable self-confidence. Indeed, one of the major goals of many of the outstanding Western schools selected for this study involves the development of self-confidence among their students. That concerted effort sets them apart from the rest of the pack. That stated goal is also one of the primary attractions to the parents of these students as well. The response to this specific question indicates that the effort is effective.

As usual, the less enthusiastic attitude of the Japanese, with over 20% responding pessimistically, and only 14.6% very positive, manifests a more modest approach to personal questions in comparison to their Western peers. It also reflects the atmosphere within their schools where little effort is made to encourage a sense of self-confidence. The one exception concerns the confidence that derives from an intense preparation in examination taking. The outstanding Japanese schools, as one of their major purposes, endeavor to build among their students the confidence that they can successfully pass the entrance examinations to the better universities. That goal is one of the major attractions to the parents who send their children to these outstanding Japanese schools.

Let there be no misunderstanding that the outstanding Japanese schools are that much different from their Western counterparts concerning this aim. Without doubt our participating American and British schools are exerting an enormous effort to instill in their students the same sense of self-confidence in passing tests that is displayed by the Japanese schools. And this effort is aimed at building the confidence to seek admission to the better universities of the land. This concern on the part of our Western schools is as appreciated by the parents there as it is in Japan. Without that, it remains doubtful if the schools in any of our three countries would continue to attract the superior students in the numbers they now do.

The self-confidence indicated among our Western students on the question above goes beyond that of examination preparation, as revealed during the interviews. An impressive number of them exhibited a general demeanor of maturity and self-confidence in handling themselves seldom demonstrated so clearly by the Japanese students. Their response to questions was forthright and direct, revealing just how accustomed they were in stating their personal opinions either about themselves or others. This is not meant to imply that their forthright opinions were always correct when relating to factual statements, for example, about Japan. In fact, their knowledge about Japan was not infrequently based on misunderstandings and errors. But their manner in stating it, right or wrong, projected a sense of personal confidence unequalled by Japan's future leaders. Our Western students, many curiously projecting a laid-back manner, nevertheless appear confident, as if they know what they are talking about. Admittedly they do have an impressive grasp of world affairs.

The modesty of the Japanese students stands in sharp contrast, reflecting what could be perceived as a lack of self-confidence not only in their answers but in themselves as well. One can pursue this line of reasoning back into the classroom itself as we did previously with other issues since many are interrelated with roots firmly imbedded in the school and society from which they originate. The self-confidence projected by our outstanding American and British students is in part an outgrowth of a classroom atmosphere in which students are expected to participate in the lesson. This takes the form of either responding to questions posed by the teacher or expressing spontaneous opinions, the latter encouraged by the typical teacher in these schools as an indication of independent thinking. It also demonstrates student interest in the subject, worthy of encouragement by the teacher, which reinforces student motivation to offer opinions.

The typical Japanese teacher in our study would not resort to such methods in the classroom. It simply is not part of the teaching methodology in Japan, nor in many other countries particularly in East Asia, it should be noted, to encourage student participation in the classroom. But again, with a class of about fifty students in the room, the atmosphere does not lend itself to active student involvement in the learning process other than note taking. Consequently our Japanese students simply do not experience the opportunity to develop a sense of self-confidence that derives from a classroom milieu that encourages students to express their opinions and have them tested publicly by actively participating in the learning process. The Japanese teacher even in these outstanding schools does not envision his or her role within that context.

To the Western observer, the outstanding schools of Japan containing large numbers of students running around fifty per classroom appear oddly out of step with modern concepts of education. However, in comparison to their Asian neighbors, where their basic cultural patterns originate, they are not that dissimilar. The same type schools in China, for example, often dubbed appropriately as "key schools," support classrooms with sixty or so students, all preparing feverishly for the entrance examinations. In Korea the very same condition exists with outstanding students crowded into the classrooms of the outstanding schools of the land. From this perspective, the Western schools are out of step with the Eastern schools.

Again, these differences between our Eastern and Western classrooms must be placed in their respective social settings. Japanese society, as we have stressed over and over again, does not encourage individual spontaneity or conspicuous display of individualism. To demonstrate a sense of strong individual confidence sets one apart from the others, a role not particularly appreciated by the others. Consequently it is not only the teacher who makes very little effort to encourage a sense of self-confidence among the students in class; the students themselves do not react favorably to the opportunity either. There is a mutuality of attitude that the classroom is not the appropriate stage for developing self-confidence among the future leaders of Japan. The response from our Japanese students, in comparison to their Western peers, is indicative of this.

In spite of this set of circumstances surrounding the education of the future leaders of Japan, which would appear to discourage the development of a sense of personal identity and self-confidence, behind that modest exterior one senses a determined figure. The society appreciates modesty and diffidence, but that is often for exterior display. The real individual that is purposely masked for social acceptability can be quite different from what appears on the surface. There is a personal determination to do one's best, to succeed, to progress, among our outstanding Japanese students that rivals the self-confidence that is so immediately visible, and impressive, with our outstanding students from America and Britain. Because of the extraordinary significance of this character trait of the future leaders of Japan, as they assume a new leadership role in the twenty-first century, the next and final chapter will consider this aspect of the research in some detail.

Characteristically, the most emphatic group among our three sets of participants exhibiting a sense of confidence in the future are the Americans, with nearly 60% anticipating a very positive future; only 0.7% harbor very pessimistic attitudes toward their personal future. Many, especially among the private sector, are ever conscious of the role their schools have played in producing more than their share of leaders of American institutions. They are literally surrounded by memorabilia reminding them of their school's past accomplishments. In addition, what has become associated with the irrepressible American character, optimism, shines through this study concerning one's personal future.

The British response is also quite positive. Again the large percentage of students enrolled in the very prestigious private British Public Schools involved in this project are also conscious of the role their schools have played in producing an inordinate number of leaders for British institutions. They, too, live their daily lives in an environment that evokes past glories of the schools. Although the overwhelming dominance their graduates were reputed to have in the past will be lessened in the governing circles of the nation in the twenty-first century, many of the contemporary students anticipate following their predecessors into the leading circles of the next century. Thus it is the much less positive attitude of the future leaders of Japan that stands in contrast.

By now we have come to anticipate a more negative response from the Japanese about their own country, in comparison to that held by our Western students toward their homeland (see Question 39). In this case,

Question 39
How do you feel about the future of the following countries?

- America -

	Very positive	Somewhat positive	Somewhat pessimistic	Very pessimistic
Americans	14.6%	51.3%	26.6%	5.5%
British	9.2	46.1	32.3	11.7
Japanese	7.4	38.2	40.2	12.8

- Britain -

	Very positive	Somewhat positive	Somewhat pessimistic	Very pessimistic
Americans	7.7	59.6	25.6	2.2
British	11.5	47.6	33.3	6.9
Japanese	6.2	46.0	36.4	7.9

- Japan -

	Very positive	Somewhat positive	Somewhat pessimistic	Very pessimistic
Americans	49.8	44.9	5.6	2.0
British	37.8	48.4	8.1	4.9
Japanese	5.6	31.9	44.4	15.5

nearly 60% of our outstanding students from Japan express pessimistic forecasts about the future of Japan. This compares to 40% of the British students who share that same opinion about Britain, and 32% of the Americans who hold a pessimistic attitude toward America's future. On the opposite side, the Americans (49.9%) and the British (37.8%) predict a very positive future for Japan, much greater than they foresee for their own country's prospects. In sharp contrast only 5.6% of the Japanese take a very positive attitude toward the future of Japan. The magnitude of the difference is impressive but understandable when the overall conditions under which these Japanese students perceive Japan in the modern world are considered. A juxtaposing of these results in various combinations aids in the appreciation of the differing perceptions (see Table 29).

From these comparisons we can more readily see how our three groups of students divide most noticeably in their assessments of Japan. Beyond that it is equally noticeable how the Japanese students take a similarly moderate attitude toward the future of all three countries. On the future of both America and Britain, the Japanese students divide almost equally between those who foresee a positive future and those who do not. On the future of Japan, the ratio is closer to 40:60 with the pessimists in the

Table 29
How do you feel about your country's future? About Japan's future?
(in parentheses)

	Very positive	Somewhat positive	Somewhat pessimistic	Very pessimistic
Americans	14.6% (49.9%)	51.3% (44.9%)	26.6% (5.6%)	5.5% (2.0%)
British	11.5 (37.8)	47.6 (48.8)	33.3 (8.1)	6.9 (4.9)
Japanese	(5.6)	(31.9)	(44.4)	(15.5

- Japanese students only -

How do you feel about the future:

	Very positive	Somewhat positive	Somewhat pessimistic	Very pessimistic
Of America?	7.4%	38.2%	40.2%	12.8%?
Of Britain?	6.2	46.0	36.4	7.9
Of Japan?	5.6	31.9	44.4	15.5

Source: Excerpted from Question 39.

majority. At least the Japanese students remain consistently cautious and somewhat pessimistic when Japan itself is under consideration.

The interviews among all three groups verified the statistical results. Most of our American students are familiar with the many commentaries depicting the relative decline of American power and prestige in the world as the twentieth century draws to a close; they are aware that the American Century may be drawing to a close as well. It should be noted that this survey was completed prior to the Middle East oil turmoil in which massive American military power was projected into the area in a very short time. However, it is unlikely that this most impressive display of military technology would significantly alter the attitudes of the rather sophisticated American students involved in this study toward the future of their country. The British students are equally aware of the impressive historical accounts of the British empire, not to be equalled again. And yet both groups anticipate a more optimistic future for their nations than the Japanese predict for the future of Japan. Moreover, the Western students perceive the future of Japan in a much more positive context than do the Japanese students.

Invariably the American and British students described the future of

Japan in superlative terms. A simple explanation by an American student summed it up succinctly: "The Japanese have their act together." The implication of this honest but frank conclusion reaches beyond the perception of the Japanese people themselves. What this student and his Western peers are implying is that the United States and Britain, once unrivaled global leaders, do not have their act together. Consequently their countries face the future with prospects less positive than Japan's.

Japanese students obviously do not envision their country's future in such glowing terms. The vast majority do not believe that their people have their act together, as it were. The very concept itself strikes them as preposterous, especially when applied to the political world. And yet they are as well informed of the new and startling entry of Japan into the exclusive club of economic superpowers as the Western students. They are constantly reminded, particularly from Western news reports, that their nation is moving upward on the ladder of national progress surpassing previous front-runners in various barometers used by Western analysts to measure national progress. Nevertheless their skepticism, disbelief if you will, that a tiny resourceless nation like Japan could attain international status in a class alongside, or even ahead of, the United States is evident in their cautious response. In a straightforward comparison of the future prospects of the three nations as perceived by the Japanese students, in every instance they rank Japan at the bottom.

The pessimistic perception of Japan and its future runs deep among the Japanese. For a nation that has traveled so far in such a short time, the general tone of disbelief is unsettling to the foreign observer. For example, in a special seminar of middle-aged middle-class Japanese women who were mostly mothers of upper school-age students, they were asked to list the positive aspects about the Japanese school system, followed by the negative features. When the time came to present their two separate lists, not one mother had listed a single positive feature about the Japanese school system that so many foreign observers come to Japan to observe. On the contrary, their lists of negative complaints were endless, such is the general attitude toward many Japanese institutions held by the Japanese themselves.

Conversely the same group of representative Japanese mothers was asked to present what they considered the positive and negative points of Western schools such as American. The general attitude took on an entirely different color. With considerable enthusiasm, they proceeded through a litany of what they perceived as the virtues of the American school. When reminded of the severe criticisms of contemporary American education by the American public, all were aware of them and agreed that there were stark and unresolved problems facing American schools. But the point is that the positive aspects come to the fore when Japanese envision Western education. The opposite takes place when they consider

Table 30
How do you feel about your country's future? Your own future?
(in parentheses)

	Very positive	Somewhat positive	Somewhat pessimistic	Very pessimistic
America	14.6% (57.9)	51.3% (36.2)	26.6% (4.1)	5.5% (0.7)
Britain	11.5 (42.9)	47.6 (48.3)	33.3 (7.1)	6.9 (1.3)
Japan	5.6 (14.6)	31.9 (62.9)	44.4 (17.1)	15.5 (4.6)

Source: Excerpted from Questions 38 and 39.

Japanese education. Our student perceptions in this survey reflect that general tone of self-criticism that permeates the society.

To return to the comparison of the perceptions our students have of their own personal future and their country's future, a rearrangement of the data from several previous questions is presented in Table 30 so that we can more fully appreciate the wide gulf between the attitudes our respondents have expressed about their future and their country's future.

In every result within the very positive category toward the future, all three nationalities believe their personal future is considerably brighter than their country's future. This is particularly evident with both the Americans and British, among whom about four times the number of students believe their own future is very positive, 51.9% and 42.9% respectively, compared with those who believe their country faces a very positive twenty-first century (14.6% and 11.5%). Even the comparable Japanese multiple is about three. When you combine the two categories of positiveness, and the two negative categories, you also derive a revealing comparison (see Table 31).

Table 31
How do you feel about your country's future? Your own future?
(in parentheses)

	Positive (very + somewhat)	Pessimistic (somewhat + very)
Americans	65.9% (94.1)	32.1% (4.8)
British	59.1 (91.2)	40.2 (8.4)
Japanese	37.5 (77.5)	59.9 (21.7)

Source: Excerpted from Questions 38 and 39.

Clearly the future leaders of these three countries are considerably more positive about their own future than their country's future, no matter how you arrange the figures. The negative responses are especially noteworthy, with few students anticipating a negative future personally but nearly 60% of the Japanese, 40% of the British, and 32% of the Americans predicting to some degree a pessimistic future for their respective countries. In other words, even though many perceive their country facing an uncertain future, these students anticipate assuming positions in it that will result in a positive future for them personally. Overall, they are much more confident of their own future than their country's future, reinforcing the conclusion that they are conscious of the role of their school in producing national and regional leaders.

Once again we note that the degree of optimism runs from the Americans at the top to the Japanese at the bottom, both in anticipating a positive future for them personally and for their country. Likewise the degree of pessimism runs from a high among the Japanese to a low among the Americans. This, of course, defies many predictions by international analysts who anticipate a further increase in Japanese influence in world affairs, commensurate with their expanding economic power. A decline in the long-term global influence of both America, despite its military superiority, and Britain, has been predicted by not a few critics who should be in a position to analyze such matters.

There is little doubt where our respondents stand on the issue presented in Question 40. The current economic superpower status of Japan is recognized by the majority of all three groups. An overwhelming number of Americans (79.2%), followed by the British (67.5%), contrasting somewhat with the lowest percentage among the Japanese (59.7%), predict Japan as the future economic leader among the three. Almost one-third of the Japanese envision the Americans maintaining their economic supremacy of the twentieth century. To the Western students, nevertheless, the twenty-first century belongs to Japan from an economic perspective. The constant stream of commentaries about Japan's economic performance in the Western media has obviously exerted a major impact on their future leaders.

Question 40
Which people will become the world's economic leaders in the twenty-first century?

	Americans	British	Japanese
The American people?	16.7%	20.4%	31.6%
The British people?	1.0	9.6	2.0
The Japanese people?	79.2	67.5	59.7

The 59.7% majority of the Japanese who chose their own country as the economic leader of the twenty-first century stands in sharp contrast to the 37.5% minority who have a positive image of their country's future, expressed in the previous set of statistics. Similarly the 65.9% majority of the Americans who believe their country has a positive future contrasts with the small minority of 16.9% who believe America will be the economic leader of the twenty-first century. This is nearly matched by the majority (59.1%) of British students who have a positive image of the nation's future, with only 9.6% believing Britain will be the dominant economic power among the three countries. There are obviously other factors in the minds of these students in their perception of the future prospects of their country.

But once again the Japanese responses may be the most interesting since the perceptions of their country's future follow diametrically divergent paths. Approximately 60% believe Japan faces a pessimistic future, while the identical number believe that Japan will become the economic leader of the twenty-first century. One could assume that these answers are incompatible. But to the Japanese they are not. The next question (Question 41) was designed to carry this line of reasoning one step further.

There is once again little doubt about the attitudes of all three groups concerning the technological leadership of the twenty-first century. To them this will be the Japanese Century technologically as well as economically. As in the previous question, the sharp contrast between the

Question 41
Which people will have the most advanced technology in the twenty-first century?

	Americans	British	Japanese
Americans?	25.8%	19.5%	14.8%
British?	0.6	5.7	0.7
Japanese?	70.2	72.5	80.0

Table 32
How do you (Japanese students) feel about your country?

Its future		As the world's future:	
Positive	Negative	Economic leaders	Technological leaders
37.3%	59.9%	59.9%	80%

Source: Excerpted from Questions 39, 40, and 41.

positive future for their country chosen by the American and British students and their choice of Japan as the leading technological nation of the future stands out. At a more extreme level, the fact that 80% of the Japanese believe their own country will become the technological leader of the twenty-first century similarly clashes with the 59.9% who hold a pessimistic perspective about the future of Japan as a nation, as presented in Table 32.

The apparent inconsistency among these results can be better understood by recalling a question from a previous chapter in which the Japanese students were asked to evaluate their political leaders. A pitifully small percentage of 1.5% expressed much confidence in their political leadership, with 77% indicating little confidence in the political leaders of the nation. In other words the Japanese students show strong faith in their economic and technological leaders but very little in their political leaders. The interviews reinforced this conclusion when students expressed pungent criticisms about how poorly the politicians were running the country. At the same time they demonstrated strong confidence in Japanese products and the nation's technological progress. The next question (Question 42) was specifically designed to shift attention from the economic to the cultural area within the same general time frame.

The cultural element produces an entirely different perspective among all three groups of outstanding students. No longer do the Japanese dominate. The twenty-first century is not considered the Japanese Century culturally. In this category a slight majority of Americans (55.9%) and British (51.1%) chose their own country as the future cultural leaders. Only the Japanese fail to select their own Oriental culture over the others. Indeed, a minority of only 23.4% perceive Japan as future cultural leaders among the three. With almost one out of two (46.1%) predicting that America will become the cultural leader of the twenty-first century, it indicates the extent of influence America plays in the life of contemporary Japan in the arts and entertainment fields that are most familiar to the teenagers involved in this study. It also reflects a cultural inferiority among the Japanese when they compare their cultural traditions with those in the West.

Question 42
Who will become the world's cultural leaders in the twenty-first century?

	Americans	British	Japanese
Americans?	55.9%	20.4%	46.1%
British?	18.8	51.1	22.8
Japanese?	19.9	25.3	23.4

Interviews among the Japanese respondents proved illuminating. To these Japanese youth their culture is, pure and simple, too unusual for Western people to understand and fully appreciate. That very perception about Japanese culture is, in fact, one of the reasons underlying the somewhat pessimistic attitudes about their nation's future. This assumption reveals that the standard the future leaders of Japan apply to evaluate their indigenous culture is basically a Western standard. In other words Japanese culture is too different from Western culture, meaning American to this generation, to be understood and appreciated in a global context. Consequently Japanese culture cannot be classified by the future leaders of Japan in the same category with either American or British culture in a global context.

It will come somewhat as a surprise to many adults in all three countries, and especially the Japanese, that one in four Americans and one in five British students predict that Japan will become the world's leader culturally in the near future. Many Japanese will find it incomprehensible that more British students (25.3%) chose Japan over America (20.4%) as the world's cultural leader in the twenty-first century. Moreover, for every two British students (51.1%) who believe their own culture will be dominant, one (25.3%) chose Japanese culture over their own in this category, a somewhat ludicrous idea to some Japanese.

A clear divergence appears on this general question (Question 43), reinforcing the general trends already evident in this chapter. Few Americans (7.2%) and British (9%) believe that the Japanese will face the most difficult circumstances in the twenty-first century. A majority of both Western groups predict that Britain is most likely to fit that unenviable category. In direct disagreement, over 45% of the Japanese students believe that Japan faces the most difficulty in meeting the challenges of the future. This, of course, contradicts their choice of Japan as the leading nation technologically (80%) and economically (59.7%) in the twenty-first century. Deep concern for the fragility of Japan, and a lack of confidence that the nation can continue to maintain its level of rapid progress, haunts these future Japanese leaders. Their lack of confidence in

Question 43
In general, which people do you think will have the most difficulty meeting the challenges of the twenty-first century?

	Americans	British	Japanese
Americans?	34.2%	27.4%	12.6%
British?	53.3	60.1	37.9
Japanese?	7.2	9.0	45.3

the current political leadership clearly represents an additional influencing factor in shaping the circumspect image of the future of the nation by this generation of Japanese youth.

The attitudes of these students toward bilateral relations in the twenty-first century, when more than a fair share of our 3,000 respondents will be involved in developing policy affecting that relationship, reflect their current perceptions (see Question 44). Although there has been considerable Japan-bashing sentiment in the United States during recent years, the future leaders of America are quite optimistic about the future ties between the two countries. Four out of five are positive, with about one in three very positive. Clearly Japan bashing in America has not had a decidedly negative influence on these outstanding students affecting their attitudes toward future relations with the Japanese people.

The Japanese, however, have a less than optimistic attitude toward the same future relationship. Only 4.8% are very positive although about 46% are, in general, positive. That still leaves just over half who are pessimistic about long-term U.S.-Japan relations. This pessimism stems in part from the more constrained attitude of the Japanese in general. It is also influenced by the public criticism from American governmental and commercial leaders toward Japanese trade policies and military expenditures during the period of this study. Japan bashing in America, seen by a few of the students as racially motivated, has exerted more of a negative

Question 44
How do you feel about the following relationships in the twenty-first century?

	– Between America and Japan –			
	Very positive	Somewhat positive	Somewhat pessimistic	Very pessimistic
Americans	29.3%	48.5%	17.6%	2.2%
Japanese	4.8	41.0	41.5	9.8
	– Between Britain and Japan –			
British	18.5%	62.2%	15.5%	1.1%
Japanese	7.1	63.0	22.5	3.6
	– Between Britain and America –			
Americans	48.2%	42.8%	5.7%	0.7%
British	48.5	40.2	7.3	2.7

influence on the future leaders of Japan than on the future leaders of America. To some Japanese the antagonistic position exhibited by certain Americans toward Japan concerning trading practices borders on the bullying. This is resented by the more sensitive youth, and some foresee potential trouble in a relationship that has proven to be very beneficial to both sides as well as to the international community.

In addition, throughout the period of this survey a number of influential Americans criticized Japan for not building up its military forces, for example, beyond 1% of gross national product. This upper limit had been commonly accepted by the governing political party and generally approved by the Japanese public at large. Few of our Japanese respondents agree with the American position, considered in more detail below. As the 1980s drew to a close, American criticism shifted somewhat to demanding considerably more financial support from the Japanese for American military bases in Japan. To the Americans, these bases have as one of their purposes the protection of Japan from any potential aggressor, meaning communist, throughout the postwar era. During the interviews the Japanese students expressed little concern about an external threat to the nation. The American position on this issue, too, has caused some resentment among our youthful Japanese. Accordingly a significant number of them envision potential trouble ahead in the bilateral relationship.

Anglo-Japanese relations are not nearly as familiar to either side as the U.S.-Japanese relationship. That familiarity, or lack of it, corresponds to the less intense but still highly significant ties between two nations located on opposite sides of the globe. Although the Japanese attitude is slightly less positive than their British counterparts, about three out of four respondents from both groups are on the optimistic side.

The results concerning future Anglo-American ties are remarkably similar and equally positive. About nine out of ten from both groups of British and Americans are positive. The so-called special relationship between two historic allies who share a common religious, linguistic, and cultural heritage will apparently continue into the twenty-first century. Among the three bilateral relationships, this one stands as the firmest. The next question (Question 45) concerning bilateral relationships with Japan confirms the fairly positive ties indicated above.

All three groups line up in nearly identical patterns on the prospect of developing future relations between Japan and the Western counterparts. It is readily understandable why the Japanese hold such a strong opinion about this question since they have a general feeling of unease about Japan's future, in which good relations with major Western powers bring a sense of comfort and security. But the most positive attitude by the Americans, in which 77.1% are in favor of developing closer relations with the Japanese, confounds the widespread media coverage in their

Question 45
Do you feel that closer relations should be developed in the twenty-first century between the following countries?

	Agree	Disagree	No opinion
— American students —			
Japan and America	77.1%	6.9%	14.0%
— British students —			
Japan and Britain	68.9	8.4	22.1
— Japanese students —			
Japan and America	69.6	13.8	13.9
Japan and Britain	69.3	8.1	20.1

country of Japan bashing. Even the Japanese students (69.6%) are not quite as enthusiastic about developing a closer relationship with America. Even so, that figure represents a very positive attitude among the Japanese group considering their generally cautious opinions on most matters.

We turn now more directly to the issue of military power, a major concern to the Japanese and Americans in the overall relationship between their countries ever since the end of World War II (see Questions 46, 47). It will surely remain an important issue into the twenty-first century. The current generation of youth has grown up in a world bristling with nuclear arms, a particularly sensitive topic in the only nation

Question 46
Attitudes toward military expenditures

Should our country increase military expenditures?

	Yes	No	No Opinion
Americans	8.3%	76.9%	14.2%
British	13.6	63.4	22.5
Japanese	8.1	76.6	13.4

Should Japan increase military expenditures?

	Yes	No	No Opinion
Americans	16.5%	56.2%	25.4%
British	5.2	64.6	29.5
(Japanese)	(8.1)	(76.6)	(13.4)

Question 47
America and Britain have nuclear weapons. Should Japan
also acquire them?

	Yes	No	No Opinion
Americans	8.0%	73.9%	16.2%
British	6.6	73.6	19.4
Japanese	7.7	85.5	6.0

that experienced the horrors of nuclear destruction. All three groups in our survey have also lived through national increases in military capability, particularly so in the United States and Japan. Indeed, during the last two decades, as the Japanese economic miracle unfolded and the financial position of the United States weakened, official American policy called for a much greater role for the Japanese armed forces to strengthen the anticommunist defenses in Asia, considered previously. Enormous pressure was exerted on the Japanese by the American government to significantly increase military spending not only in the buildup of Japanese forces, which has taken place, but in the financial support to offset the high costs of maintaining American army, navy, air force, and marine bases operating on Japanese soil. This, too, has been met to a substantial degree.

Even though there has been a relaxation of tension throughout the Far East, to the extent that even the North and South Korean governments are testing the waters of negotiation, the magnitude of Japanese military power will conceivably become even more of an issue in the twenty-first century as the buildup continues. The most recent topic of great interest and concern both within Japan and abroad involves the possibility of deploying Japanese military forces overseas in international contingencies such as the Middle East. Our survey, however, was completed before this proposal took substantive form. The future leaders who will most likely be involved in influencing policy on these critical issues were asked to respond to several of the very basic questions surrounding the topic of military preparedness. For comparative purposes, all respondents were asked the same general questions.

There is a convergence of opinion among the 3,000 participants from three countries on these fundamental questions concerning military strength (Question 46). Manifestly it runs against their respective governments' positions during the past decade. In particular American policy, concentrating its efforts to induce a seemingly reluctant Japan to rearm by substantially increasing its military expenditures, received little support from the future leaders of each country. However, they all go well beyond that. Only about one in ten approve a further military buildup in their own country. Their strong opposition to Japanese nuclear arms (Question 47), in which the Western students stand shoulder to shoulder with their Japanese peers, mirrors a general attitude toward military expenditures.

Of major importance is the reaction of our future Japanese leaders to the gradual shift in American foreign policy toward Japan's military position. Where once the primary emphasis was placed on the buildup of Japanese military power to help defend their island nation, recent demands by the Americans concentrate more on an increase in Japanese financing of American military bases in Japan, mentioned previously. The goal is to offset the very high costs of maintaining a substantial American military presence from northern Japan through the southern islands of Okinawa. Included are two giant air bases and an aircraft carrier group all located in the greater Tokyo area, where the cost of living may be the highest in the world. Japanese students revealed during the interviews that they strongly oppose this indirect increase in their country's military expenditures as well, whether it is earmarked for a Japanese buildup or to finance American forces within Japan. Their concern about the future relations between the two nations is related to these divergent attitudes toward the need for any further strengthening of military power regardless of its nature. The American students, in principle, agree with this attitude.

The similarity among the three nationalities in their answers to Question 48 comes as somewhat of a surprise. One could expect a common reaction to this question by American and British students, who have little knowledge of the state of Japan's military forces. But Japanese students, mindful of the continuing military buildup of the so-called Japanese defense forces during the two-year period of this study, could arguably hold a stronger attitude of concern toward a potential rebirth of Japanese militarism than their Western counterparts. Nevertheless the visibility of the Japanese military in daily affairs, including political activities, is greatly restricted so that few of our Japanese students know much about their armed forces. Their major source of information comes from the

Question 48
In your opinion, how likely is a rebirth of Japanese militarism?

	Very likely	Fairly likely	Not likely
Americans	5.6%	38.5%	50.9%
British	7.6	32.9	56.6
Japanese	7.5	35.7	55.2

media, where the topic was not given that much coverage during this survey. Regardless of the nearly identical responses by the three sets of participants, there is significance in the fact that nearly half of the 3,000 students from three countries still hold some concern about the Japanese in terms of militarism.

In a world equipped with thousands of nuclear missiles, any one of them capable of massive destruction, the fact that so few students from three distinct areas of the world fear a nuclear war in their lifetime is quite a remarkable commentary on world affairs (see Question 49). It may be considered even more impressive since our students responded to this question and were interviewed before and during the sudden collapse of the Eastern European communist bloc, which greatly eased international tensions. Even in Japan, where the atomic bombings of World War II are remembered annually in so many ways, only one in five students are concerned about nuclear warfare. This generation of youth may be the first since Hiroshima to feel a sense of security despite the prevalence of nuclear weapons in the world.

There is considerable ambivalence among all our groups about the prospects of world peace in the twenty-first century (see Question 50). Between one in ten to one in twenty were very positive or very pessimistic about future peace. The majority from all three countries fell within the broad center. Being conscious of world history replete with warfare, and

Question 49
Do you think there will be a nuclear war during your lifetime that will involve your country?

	Yes	No	No opinion
Americans	9.9%	64.5%	24.7%
British	9.1	65.1	25.0
Japanese	20.5	37.7	40.5

Question 50
How do you feel about world peace in the twenty-first century?

	Very positive	Somewhat positive	Somewhat pessimistic	Very pessimistic
Americans	12.6%	35.9%	29.3%	20.7%
British	15.3	42.6	25.4	15.5
Japanese	6.5	41.3	37.1	12.4

aware of the many localized wars and areas of tension, our future leaders exhibited a sense of caution and skepticism about peace during their lifetime. The interviews reinforced this ambivalence. Curiously, for the first time the Japanese were less dissimilar from their Western counterparts than usual, while the Americans were uncharacteristically pessimistic. Again it must be noted that the survey was conducted before the Middle East crisis which led to war, with victorious American forces in the forefront. The general concern expressed in the interviews about the decline of the influence and power of America in the future underlay the cautious attitude by the American students about future world peace, in which the United States was perceived as no longer in a position to maintain stability on a global level.

In general about half of our students in each country are optimistic and the other half pessimistic about world peace in the twenty-first century, when many of them will assume leadership positions. As outstanding students in their respective countries, they have studied world history rather intensively. Although none of them personally experienced wartime, there was a certain feeling of anxiety as to whether the prolonged period of global peace the world experienced following World War II could be sustained, from an historical perspective. "Can it last forever? I doubt it." That simple expression of concern sums up the position taken by many of the pessimists, prophetic as it turned out. The optimists took heart in the belief that the cold war was coming to an end, and with it the bipolar division of the world since World War II, leading to a sustainable era of peace.

The polarization of opinions among the future leaders of major countries concerning world peace in the twenty-first century, between the half who anticipate world peace during that era and the other half who do not, may in itself be a positive sign. One could argue that influential nations need optimistic leaders with positive thinking about the future. Conversely others could argue that, based on historical precedent, those who are concerned that peace remains a fragile commodity should be part of the decision-making process, assuming their concern heightens an awareness of the inevitable dangers to the maintenance of peace in the twenty-first century.

This, then, leads to our final chapter: the issue of leadership itself in the twenty-first century, as it relates to the challenges facing those who will be making the decisions that determine the direction of modern civilization. Specifically, our focus concerns how the future Japanese leaders will respond to those unprecedented challenges and the responsibilities they entail, as Japan assumes its new position among the world's foremost nations.

7

LEADERSHIP FOR THE TWENTY-FIRST CENTURY

Japan's New Role

During the last half of the twentieth century, international leadership has been dominated by those countries that projected military power throughout vast areas of the world. Regardless of the quality of the leaders that emerged from these military superpowers, their influence was sustained, as it were, by the number and range of their nuclear arsenals. International relations were deeply imbedded in military strategy that divided the world essentially into two military blocs. The leaders of the two, the United States and the Soviet Union, assumed global leadership to a great extent by virtue of their military superiority.

With the unexpectedly rapid dissolution of the Eastern European communist bloc, the military supremacy of its leader, the USSR, has been seriously undermined, casting doubt on its military capability and reliability. The global projection of Soviet power has consequently been seriously eroded. At some point in the continuing process the classification of the Soviet Union as a world leader based on military power will come into question. To some analysts, it already has.

In reaction to the military force reductions of the Soviet Union, the other twentieth-century bloc leader, the United States, initiated a reduction of its military power. Economic constraints hastened the process, as it decidedly has in the USSR as well, with both global leaders realistically addressing a deterioration of their economic foundations. Nevertheless the so-called oil crisis in the Middle East in the early 1990s resulted in a rapid deployment and use of massive American power into that area, demonstrating quite clearly that America still maintained a mighty military capability. The action also demonstrated that the United States could no longer finance large-scale military actions by itself without unacceptably damaging its financial system. It sought enormous financial support from other countries, including Japan, to pay the bill. These events indicate that by the twenty-first century the two super-powers of the twentieth century may be unable to forge understandings that determine regional issues formerly contained by their military superiority.

A new criterion for entry into world leadership ranks is emerging. Pundits argue that, at the turn of the century, military might will not automatically qualify a nation's leaders as international leaders vested with influence that extends around the globe. Instead, economic power is evolving as one of the most prominent factors in the equation for entry into the select class of world leaderhip. The control of money with all of its profound ramifications, rather than the number and range of nuclear arsenals and all that entails, will be a primary factor determining the extent of global influence a nation's leaders can exert.

The new order of priorities places Japan in an unaccustomed and highly strategic position in world affairs in the twenty-first century. As a second-rate military power under a self-imposed nuclear ban in the twentieth century, the nation did not fully qualify as a world power with leaders exerting a major influence on international affairs. However, applying the new yardstick for determining global influence, Japan finds itself as, for example, the world's major creditor as well as donor nation, backing into the exalted ranks of world leadership. That new position will entitle Japanese leaders to greatly influence decisions that will affect us all by the turn of the century, a process well under way. How they respond to this new opportunity to exert global influence is our primary concern.

We have developed through this study a profile of the perceptions and attitudes of many of the future leaders of Japan, as well as their schools, who will be in a position to make those decisions of global importance in the twenty-first century. And we have, wherever possible, juxtaposed that profile against a profile of the future leaders and their schools from the two nations that experienced global leadership in the nineteenth and twentieth centuries and whose outstanding schools continue a tradition of developing leadership qualities among its students. The similarities and differences in the responses provide us with the material to make comparative analyses.

We are now in a position to address the major question that prompted this study in the first place. Will Japan be capable of providing effective international leadership commensurate with its economic power in the twenty-first century? Will its future leaders, many of them sitting in the classrooms of the nation's outstanding schools at this very moment, command the respect of the international community expected of leaders from nations that have attained international prominence? In a word, will Japan's national leaders attain the status of, and be recognized as, responsible international leaders in the twenty-first century?

The burden on Japan to provide international leadership is particularly difficult to achieve for two major reasons. The first inevitably concerns the nation's geographical limitations, a factor forever in the back of the Japanese mind since their daily lives are a constant reminder of that unavoidable condition, but which others tend to ignore from their external perspective. Japan resembles the British position of the nineteenth century in which a tiny resourceless island nation endeavored to extend its power and influence around the world. The global British empire of a former era accomplished that remarkable feat, attributed by pundits to a significant extent to the ability of a small number of graduates from the British Public Schools, including the very institutions involved in this study. However, it was achieved at a period of world history when civilization was essentially based on agrarian economies. There was also little competition from large and powerful nation-states like the United States and the USSR, with which the Japanese must contend for global influence. It is, without doubt, far more difficult in the twenty-first century for any small island nation like Japan to achieve superpower status similar to that of the British in the nineteenth century.

The second major obstacle for Japan to overcome, which neither the British nor the Americans faced in their ascendancy to world leadership, relates to the fact that Japan is an Oriental country with Oriental traditions. International diplomacy and intercourse are essentially based on Western traditions and codes of conduct. Japan may be a world leader in high technology and modern electronics. It remains, nevertheless, an Oriental-based society, with traditional features cherished by Oriental people for centuries prior to their exposure to modern Western concepts of nationhood and international diplomacy, business, and commerce.

The contemporary patterns of leadership that originate from Japan reflect the feudal remnants of traditional social patterns adapted to the modern demands of highly industrialized societies. For example, the custom of loyalty to the company exhibited by the overwhelming majority of Japanese employees, even in the highest of high tech industries, reflects relationships reminiscent of a bygone era. In this part of the world, behavioral traits that govern relationships between individuals, groups, and institutions are commonly attributed to the continuing influence of Confucian teachings, originated in China, that once dominated Japanese culture.

The educational system of modern Japan, including the outstanding schools of the land, is similarly fashioned from the demands of an industrialized society, originated in the West, on an Oriental foundation of hierarchical relationships that have withstood the test of time. For example, the classroom atmosphere exhibits characteristics of the ancient learning process with the sage, recognized as such by the students who stand briefly before him at the opening of class, passing on to the next generation the wisdom of the ages. But the very fact that Japan has been able to achieve international prominence in the most advanced areas of high technology such as lasers, in spite of its traditional social and educational patterns, is not only a remarkable achievement; it understandably renders the Japanese cautious in attempting to reform or internationalize the system. Internationalization, a popular slogan among the Japanese media, is, in fact, a current euphemism often substituted for westernization in which rational thinking and action replaces traditionally accepted patterns of behavior among people and institutions based on age, station, and gender, among other factors.

In recent years there has been some controversy among both foreign observers and the Japanese themselves surrounding the concept of the uniqueness of Japanese culture. In actuality, this means uniquely different from Western, often American, culture. There is surely a basis for concluding that indeed Japanese culture is distinctly different from most others, and especially American, as the Americans or the Chinese or the Indians believe their culture is likewise uniquely different from others. Our Japanese students feel this instinctively. One revealed a common attitude that was alluded to in an earlier chapter when he concluded that Japan could never be the cultural leader of the twenty-first century since it is too different from the West to become internationally prominent. Again this representative from the future class of Japanese leaders applied a Western, mostly American, standard to judge his own culture. The two are naturally, and decidedly, different, originating from two vastly different historical settings.

But this is similarly true with many, if not most, non-Western societies that developed indigenous cultural patterns long before European influence spread throughout the world. What makes the Japanese experience unique is not the cultural differences, but rather that Japan is the first non-Western society to attain international influence economically with which Western leaders must directly compete, not only in the international arena but at home as well. For the first time in modern history Western countries that had maintained economic supremacy for centuries, enabling them to extend their cultural influence throughout the world and setting the patterns for international intercourse, must deal with non-Western people, the Japanese, as equals. It is somewhat baffling to both sides as they increasingly share responsibility for global leadership.

The demanding task the Japanese face involves producing national leaders that fit traditional indigenous patterns of acceptability who must then be able to adapt to Western patterns of acceptability at the international level. And they are decidedly not the same. In other words, Japan's leaders who represent the nation in the international arena must of necessity first make it to the top of Japanese institutions according to Japanese traditions. They then find it necessary to change course and adapt to Western patterns of international relationships, language, and conduct. They must negotiate and bargain with Western leaders who have come from Western educational institutions with a history of educating leaders who confidently step into the leadership class, not infrequently following in the footsteps of their fathers and, to a lesser extent, their mothers.

The latter fact itself represents just one of the very difficult features of Western societies Japanese leaders must contend with in international affairs. Increasingly women are included as representatives of Western countries either in international organizations or, in the case of trade negotiations with the United States, even as the chief negotiator. In one particular instance the American female leader projected a commanding presence making strident demands on the Japanese and inflicting a barrage of criticism of their so-called intransigent attitudes. Sitting across from a female leader representing a superpower at the bargaining table, and treating her as an equal if not more than an equal, was an uncommon experience for Japanese leaders. They are simply unaccustomed to women in decision-making positions of responsibility in government, industry, and most other sectors of the society as well. In this case, according to one of the Japanese leaders who sat across from the formidable female American leader, the Japanese soon got used to dealing with her since she sounded like so many of the American male leaders. They simply treated her like a man.

This places the outstanding schools of Japan, which are educating more than their share of the future leaders of the nation out of whom originate much of the international leadership, in a particularly sensitive and vulnerable position. First of all, the teachers and administrators of these schools, most of them males teaching mostly males, are certainly not versed in international conduct, nor do many of them possess a broad outlook on life. They happen to be teaching the future leaders of the nation solely by virtue of their mastery of one narrow subject area and the skill to present it so that their students have a far better than average chance to pass the university entrance examination in that subject. Their qualifications seldom go beyond that single criterion.

This does not mean that character and personality are ignored in the selection of new teachers for Japan's outstanding schools. Seriousness of purpose and dedication are all part of the overall qualifications the schools are looking for in the new teacher. But those characteristics relate directly to the responsibility of the teacher in preparing the students for the entrance examinations in a particular area of teaching. And the teachers in these schools fulfill those criteria most effectively. They are, for the most part, highly dedicated and serious in their responsibility for educating many of Japan's future leaders in their subject area.

One could be excused for expecting at least foreign language teachers, invariably English, to perhaps have some experience abroad or at least be able to converse respectably in the international language of English. That is usually not the case. The capability to speak English does not noticeably enhance the English teacher's ability to prepare the students for the university entrance examinations, nearly always requiring the translation of English passages into Japanese or the choice of given answers to detailed and sometimes bizarre grammatical questions. In an odd sense, the ability to speak English may exert an inhibiting influence on an English teacher's skill in preparing the students for the English examination. One who speaks the language would seldom view it in such an unnatural manner. One who speaks it would tend to use it during the English class, not viewed as particularly helpful. In other words the teachers and administrators of Japan's outstanding schools are neither prepared, nor expected to serve, as role models for the future leaders of Japan in an international context.

It would be ideal if Japanese schools could aim for critical thinking, innovative ideas, creativity, originality, and so on, similar to the aims of our corresponding Western schools. But the system does not allow it. As we have seen, the outstanding schools of Japan are deeply immersed in the competition for entry of their students into the major universities, requiring a great deal of effort in learning factual information and test-taking devices for ultimate success. One could conclude that the schools we are dealing with exacerbate the situation. They encourage their students to completely apply themselves to pass the tests, rendering it more difficult for their competitors to surpass them as examination test constructors gradually increase the level of difficulty as students increase their ability to pass them. To expect graduates of this system to pass through it successfully and suddenly flower into visionary internationalists is illogical in this century, and the next.

These conditions apply not only to Japan, as noted. They apply to all non-Western societies, particularly those without a colonial history in which the schools were patterned after European schools producing natives that have a Western orientation who can fit rather comfortably into the international community, both in habit and language. Most Japanese leaders are ill prepared at both, and find Western customs that prevail at the international level oftentimes incompatible with Japanese traditions. Many find the experience uncomfortable. It is one of the major factors in the short-term assignments of Japanese to overseas posts in international organizations.

The United Nations represents a perfect example of the situation.

Because of the increase in the Japanese contribution to the UN, it qualifies for a proportional increase in permanent employees. However, periodically UN personnel recruiters must personally travel to Japan seeking Japanese nationals to fill their staff quotas allocated according to, as it were, financial power. They have yet to reach the goal. The unfilled Japanese quotas must by default be filled by nationals from other countries whose financial status seldom matches that of Japan. The UN experience may be a harbinger of the twenty-first century in which Japan, by default, fails to assume the international leadership role entitled to it corresponding to its financial status.

The protracted negotiations between Japan and the United States over trading practices represent one of many examples of the problems Japanese leaders face at the international level. The American negotiators, in one case led by a woman described earlier, insisted on direct responses to their persistent demands, and they wanted them quickly. Strident criticisms were sprinkled throughout the negotiations, repeated later on nationwide television dutifully translated into Japanese in the various gradations of politeness for which the language is noted. The leaders of Japan, many of them coming through the better schools where student leaders were successful harmonizers of groups rather than major decision makers, could not produce quick responses to suit the American side. A consensus is not always readily achieved. And when the Japanese side is unable to harmonize the various opinions on very sensitive and controversial issues such as opening up the domestic rice markets to imports, decisions are delayed until a consensus can be forged.

The Americans want prompt responses regardless of the consequences to the Japanese side when they feel they have proven their position factually, beyond a reasonable doubt. The virtual ban on rice imports fits into that category. The Japanese think in terms of human relationships and cannot come to painful decisions that are unacceptable to various groups. They then want to postpone the fateful decision, endeavoring to fashion a compromise palatable to all sides, often a time-consuming process.

The Americans interpret delay as a deliberate provocation of stalling. The prevalent attitude among American leaders is that the only way to provoke the Japanese into action, which means accepting American demands or compromising to the degree acceptable to the American side, is to apply the utmost pressure in the most visible public manner. Unaccustomed to such overt negotiating tactics at home, where subtleties of style govern relationships, the Japanese are often at a loss, scrambling for a face-saving formula that gives the Americans the minimum they will accept. That response then confirms to the Americans the wisdom of their strategy and style in dealing with Japanese leaders, to be repeated at the next opportunity.

One of our Japanese students summed up the dilemma their leaders face on the international front. When the students choose their school leaders for presidents of clubs, the qualifications they want relate primarily to the ability to organize the members into a harmonious group. The student who is most skilled at keeping harmony among the members is considered the most successful. The members are much less concerned with their leader's ability to represent them to the outside. Their criterion for effective leadership is how the student handles himself, and in these outstanding schools the leaders are overwhelmingly boys, in harmonizing the other members of the group. In a sense they do not want someone to lead them who has a broad perspective and takes bold action accordingly, but one who concentrates primarily on their group, shaping it into a harmonious whole. This is the kind of domestic training Japan's future leaders experience, and must master, before they can assume responsibility on an international level. However, at that level, where their foreign counterparts are often American, given the major role the United States plays in Japan's international relations, the rules and codes of conduct are vastly different.

The business world, where Japanese leaders are taking an ever-increasing role at the international level, presents particularly appropriate situations that illustrate the dilemma of Japanese leadership in concrete terms. A member of this writer's weekly seminar, the president of a very successful high tech company of 3,000 employees, came under pressure to enter into a joint venture with an American company, the largest in the world in this particular industry. It was, therefore, the Japanese firm's major global competitor. The joint venture proposal was passed through the various offices and layers of responsibility of the Japanese company and finally reached the president himself, with the cautious recommendation that it be considered favorably. He would not act unless a broad consensus among his staff had been attained. But there was concern among them that the American company was merely trying to enter the Japanese market, dominated by this Japanese firm, through a joint venture.

The American chairman was a no-nonsense businessman who, easily angered, spoke directly and to the point, intimidating the Japanese president on previous encounters. In the very final session, which ran on for hours, the American chairman demanded that the Japanese president make his position absolutely clear. The Japanese deferred by suggesting that the American side make the initial concrete offer and the Japanese would react. In the process there were rather unpleasant encounters that upset the American chairman, which he made no effort to conceal. There were other times when the Japanese side concealed certain concerns because they feared it would upset the American leader even further. The session was marked by breaks in the negotiations when the Japanese president felt it necessary to confer with his staff. All in all it was a very trying experience for the Japanese, in part because of communication difficulties in English, in which nuances apparently confused the Japanese side on occasion.

In the end the Japanese accepted the American proposal of a fifty-fifty joint venture in which the Japanese assumed that the American side would act fairly in areas of dispute, since neither side commands the majority position. An interesting sidelight is that the final offer by the American side surprised the Japanese since the joint venture offer had been revised to cover only America and Europe, not Japan. In fact, as revealed after the signing, the Americans were trying primarily to avoid direct competition with the Japanese company in America and Europe. They feared that, in the long run, the Japanese would outcompete them on their home grounds. In the final analysis the Japanese president led his delegation successfully back to Japan because of the competitive power of his company, not because of a carefully designed plan employing skilled negotiating techniques.

The dilemma confronting Japanese leaders in the twenty-first century is not a new phenomenon. It has been a recurring theme throughout the modern history of Japan. When the nation first faced westward in the latter half of the 1800s, the chief diplomat posted to Washington, Mori Arinori, fit in too comfortably with American political and particularly intellectual leaders. A progressive intellectual himself, later to become the father of Japan's modern school system before being murdered by a fanatical nationalist for his Western proclivities, Mori was an international diplomat of the first order both in language and persuasion. In an attempt to lead Japan into the modern world, meaning Western, from its feudal customs, he became too much of an internationalist. A delegation of Japanese leaders visiting Washington under Mori's guidance reportedly complained to higher officials, upon returning home, about his strange manners and actions as a Japanese government official. In essense he had become too Western. He was shortly thereafter recalled, terminating what could have been an enlightened period of early Japanese-American relationships under a rare internationalist leader from Japan.

The most recent and revealing example of Japan's inability to assume a leadership role in international affairs has taken place during the Gulf War. This nation, among leading countries of the world, is most dependent on oil imported from the troubled Middle East. Accordingly, its government came under enormous international pressure to provide major support for a coalition of nations under American leadership fighting for control of strategic oil reserves in the area. Struggling to achieve an internal consensus, Japan's leaders exhibited a sense of caution and indecision reflecting their reticence to assume an international role commensurate with their financial power. Characteristically, the government finally contributed substantial financial support, bowing to powerful American pressure. Remaining awkwardly quiet in the wings, however, the Japanese were distant observers while a major international episode—with major economic ramifications for them—was staged. The Japanese were, in fact, conspicuously absent from the decision-making process that affected so much of the world dependent upon an oil-based economy.

Many Japanese students are acutely conscious of the narrowness of their education and their limited perspective as a result of it. One of the senior boys from a leading school, the chairman of the student association, revealed an image shared by many when he said that he simply could not imagine Japanese leaders assuming an international role alongside American leaders in the twenty-first century. This same student also confirmed his confidence in getting a leading position either in government service or private industry within Japan. He had little confidence in himself going beyond that level, although he was chosen as the leader of the entire student association at one of the most famous high schools in Japan. What he was revealing was his confidence in becoming a national leader, but not an international leader.

The twenty-first-century leaders of America and Britain currently studying in the outstanding schools of their countries do not face the future prospect of adapting to a double identity, one appropriate for domestic institutions and the other markedly different for international concourse. For those who eventually participate in the latter at the commercial or governmental level, their code of conduct will not differ markedly in the international arena from that they practiced at the national level. For example, when American leaders participate in negotiations with the Japanese in Japan, their manners, actions, and behavior are not dissimilar to top-level meetings at home. To the extent possible, they demonstrate initially a relaxed aura, with good-natured humor intended to reduce the ceremonial ritual the Japanese are accustomed to at formal meetings at home. Then the time for serious business takes place with direct and not infrequently confrontational exchanges ensuing in the give-and-take of negotiations.

The instant informality of the American representatives strikes the Japanese awkwardly since relationships in their country reach the informal stage only after considerable personal association in informal settings. The use of first names that Americans prefer, for example, the George and Toshiki relationship struck up by President Bush and Prime Minister Kaifu, was received with some perplexity and amusement by the Japanese. Colleagues within the same institution, particularly at the senior levels, often do not call each other by their first names, let alone a nickname, even after years of close association. In this writer's academic department of a university in Tokyo, for example, Japanese colleagues who have worked together for thirty years still call each other only by their last names with an appropriate prefix of Mr. or professor. One can rest assured that no Japanese government official or fellow politician called Prime Minister Kaifu "Toshiki" under any circumstance. That custom is only acceptable at the international level if the American side follows it. The savvy Japanese politicians, admittedly, exploit it for the home audience as an indication of their leader's ability to forge a special relationship with the United States, the cornerstone of Japanese foreign policy.

The future leaders of America and Britain are receiving an education that prepares them to become effective leaders at both the domestic level, either regionally or nationally, as well as the international level. They have, of course, the advantage of growing up in societies that developed the basic patterns of international relations which evolved from indigenous customs. Many of their predecessors from the same schools, in fact, were instrumental in setting those very patterns. And throughout, the language they use at home and school will be the primary language used for international affairs. Fortunately for them English has become the most acceptable language in the international arena.

But beyond that, these outstanding schools in America and Britain make a major effort to instill leadership capability, and the confidence to go with it, that has applicability at both the domestic and international levels. In other words the future leaders from both America and Britain are far more adequately prepared for international leadership than are the Japanese, having been educated in many of the schools that served that role for years. Their graduates are much more at home in the international forum than the Japanese are, knowing that many of the graduates from their schools have gone before them and that the rules are governed by traditions and customs that are familiar to them and their teachers.

This is not to infer that the outstanding schools of Japan are ill-equipped to prepare their graduates for effective leadership in the twenty-first century. On the contrary, they are. However, the distinction must be made between domestic leadership and international leadership. The accomplishments of our schools participating in this study, representative of the outstanding sector of schools in Japan, demonstrate that far more than their share of graduates enter the better universities. This naturally positions them for better employment choices, placing them within striking distance of the leadership class. Because these graduates are not only bright but immensely motivated, as demonstrated by their zeal and effort to get into these schools and into the better if not the very best universities, they are well prepared to assume leadership of Japanese institutions that are patterned on traditional social patterns. And the vast majority still are.

The system, including the outstanding schools, remains in place because it has served the nation well with its spectacular economic miracle of the twentieth century. There can be little doubt that Japan's outstanding schools have already accomplished a remarkable feat in preparing a generation of postwar youth, following the devastating military defeat, that has effectively participated in that process. The teachers, administrators, and particularly the graduates of these schools take great pride in that accomplishment.

But the twenty-first century presents new challenges to the Japanese in which their economic influence at the international level entitles them to assume a much greater international role befitting their economic stature. They can no longer be classified as a second-rate power as they were during a previous era, judged primarily on military might. Accordingly their outstanding schools should conceivably be undergoing major changes that would equip them to prepare their graduates for the international challenges many of them will undoubtedly face as leaders of one of the major nations in the world. This would entail a drastically different atmosphere in the classroom and in the general goals and purposes of the school itself. There is, however, little evidence that either is taking place or seriously being contemplated for the near future, certainly not by the turn of the century.

On the other hand, there are some who take a different perspective on the reformation and internationalization of Japanese education. They question whether the outstanding Japanese schools should become domestic versions of the venerable Eton and Andover, Harrow and Hotchkiss, or the fine public schools such as Stuyvesant in New York City and the Oratory School in London. This position invites further critical questions. Can Japan assume a leading international role in the twenty-first century without radically reforming its educational institutions more on the lines of the outstanding schools in the West? Are there aspects of Japanese culture and traditions that should be maintained regardless of their consequences on Japan's role in international affairs?

To rephrase the question from the opposite angle, are there features of Japanese culture and education that will not only serve Japan well domestically, as they apparently have or a nation with such restrictive geographical limitations could not have reached the status it has during the twentieth century; but could those same features also serve the nation well at the international level, enabling Japan to assume a responsible role in the twenty-first century appropriate to its economic position?

The ultimate issue, then, is whether the outstanding schools of contemporary Japan, following traditional patterns of teaching and learning, are adequately preparing many of the future leaders of the nation for responsible leadership at both the domestic and the international levels in the twenty-first century. Since there appears little attempt under way to make significant changes, the question is not a mere theoretical exercise. It is the reality that the Japanese themselves should be grappling with. If the answer is basically affirmative, then we all benefit since the economic influence of Japan has a global impact. If, on the other hand, the conclusion is negative, the adverse effects will also exert a global impact, such is the consequence of Japan's international role in the twenty-first century.

In order to draw some basic conclusions about this critical issue, this researcher during the two years of the study visited representative outstanding schools that participated in the project, interviewing administrators, teachers, and students from both the public and the private sectors in all three countries. Those experiences proved enlightening as well as invaluable. The conclusions drawn here are also based on a lifetime in the field of education in which Japan, America, and Britain have played an integral role. This includes experiences as an American public school teacher after going through the American education system, completing graduate study at one of Britain's foremost universities, and pursuing a thirty-year career teaching in the Division of Education at a distinguished university in Japan serving as chairman of the Graduate Faculty of Education for part of that time.

There are indeed enduring qualities in Japan's outstanding schools that have and will continue to exert a positive influence on the future leaders of the nation, both for domestic and for international leadership. Many of them cannot be measured statistically nor judged by physical appearances. They have served the nation well in the postwar period. There is no reason to think they cannot serve Japan well in the twenty-first century as the country emerges as one of the major nations in the world. This certainly does not mean that some adjustments in priorities would not be beneficial. Every institution can be improved. However, any profound changes in the system could undermine the basic infrastructure of the society that enabled Japan to attain world status under the harshest conditions in the first place. A fundamental revision of Japan's outstanding schools could conceivably erode the foundation for its continuation.

We begin with a concept that has received much attention from this writer in other contexts: that of *gambare*, or perseverance. The spirit of perseverance or determination has been a hallmark of the Japanese character from the distant past. The Japanese have endured immense sacrifice to achieve a goal, whether it be physical or mental. It has been associated in more recent times with the national effort to catch up with the West in the process of modernizing Japanese society and industry. This tradition has developed into a cultural trait that adheres to the principle of perfectibility: that everyone, not just the nation, possesses the potential for improvement; that everyone can succeed at achieving their goals if they persevere through adversity; that, in a word, everyone is perfectible.

The outstanding Japanese schools in this study obviously did not develop this cultural trait. Rather, they reflect it, and perfect it, by bringing together the brightest students, fully dedicated teachers, and a

simple environment that literally enables the students to perfect themselves. In this instance it is the goal to perfect oneself in the examination
preparation process that the society has accepted as the ultimate symbol
of success. And perseverance is the cornerstone of it all. For example, one
cannot imagine the future leaders of America and Britain in our outstanding schools, who are also undergoing a rigorous academic university
preparatory course, further enrolling in supplementary courses with
demanding requirements outside their regular school hours. At least half
of the students who enter Tokyo University, for example, have spent one
full year or more after completing the very demanding high school course
in further preparation for that fateful examination. And those courses are
not inexpensive. Nevertheless it exemplifies the individual's attempt to
perfect himself at personal sacrifice.

Perseverance at personal sacrifice is the embodiment of Japan's postwar
economic miracle. The older generation reveres the concept of *gambare*,
which enabled them to survive the wartime destruction of their country
and undertake the herculean effort to successfully rebuild it. They make
every attempt to instill the personal ethic of perseverance in the young,
obviously not always possible. In fact what deeply concerns many of
Japan's older generation of leaders is that the current generation of youth,
the first to be brought up amidst Japan's postwar prosperity, will
succumb to an affluent style of life that could erode the spirit of *gambare*
when a sacrificial effort no longer appears necessary.

Observing the students in these outstanding schools educating many of
the future leaders of the nation, that concern seems unfounded, or at least
premature. There is an inner compulsion driving our Japanese students to
seek perfectibility in the one major challenge before them, the entrance
examination. Their effort at great personal sacrifice resembles the earlier
Japanese who sacrificed to enable Japan to catch up with the West and, in
some instances, even surpass their Western competitors. The enduring
spirit of *gambare*—perseverance—will serve the future leaders of Japan
well at both the national and the international levels. It may even be
contagious.

But our statistics tell another story. The young people of Japan who will
become the leaders of the twenty-first century are clearly not convinced
that Japan has caught up with the West, at least not to the extent that
would warrant a relaxation of effort. Indeed the opposite is true. One of
the most significant results of this study demonstrates that nearly half of
the 1,000-plus Japanese participants believe that Japan faces the most
difficulty meeting the challenges of the twenty-first century. Only 12%
place America in that unfortunate position.

To our future leaders of Japan, the race to catch up is far from over.
The competition remains under way, and the Japanese continue to run
behind the leader. America is perceived as the front-runner. The

challenge to catch up remains a strong motivating influence on this generation of outstanding youth as it did to a previous generation. The Japanese boy destined for leadership, who could not imagine his country's leaders in the same class as American leaders, reinforces the standard image of the challenge America presents to the Japanese, regardless of the new economic and technological advances of the nation. Even though a vast majority of the Japanese students foresee their nation as the twenty-first-century leader economically and technologically, they cannot yet envision Japan as a world class leader in the same league with America.

If perceptions acquired by the teenage level are generally carried over into adulthood, as research quoted in the first chapter indicates, then we can make certain predictions about the leaders of Japan in the twenty-first century. They may recognize their country as most advanced in certain areas but not able to join the same league as the United States in exerting global leadership. The unforgettable image of Japan as a small resourceless island nation curtails any vision of international supremacy. Even during the expansionist era of militaristic aggression of the 1930s and 1940s, there were many Japanese who recognized the folly of it all. That sense of realism pervades this generation of outstanding students. It will be an influential factor in their conduct as leaders of Japan in the twenty-first century.

This, then, leads to the next trait of the outstanding schools of Japan: the challenge of competition. Ironically, in a society based on group relations, there is an enormous effort to instill into every succeeding generation an intense spirit of competition, both individually and corporately. It sustains the industrial competitiveness of Japanese industry. It pervades every aspect of the school, both in and out of the classroom. Within the classroom it relates directly to the individual challenge of successfully passing the entrance examination not to any university, which is common to about 35% of the entire age level, but to the better if not the most famous institutions in the land beginning with Tokyo University. The statistical fact that a number of our participating schools place into Tokyo University anywhere from 50 to 150 students per year, including direct graduates and those entering after an additional year of study, proves just how successful these schools are in challenging their students to compete academically at the highest competitive level in the nation. It is a challenge to the competitiveness of the individual.

Equally competitive are the nonacademic activities of the school that develop a group spirit of competition, honed through sports. In a school that is dominated by university academic preparation, the role of sports is little appreciated nor understood outside the system. In fact, as in our outstanding Western schools, sports play an essential role in the preparation of the future leaders of the country. It is all centered on the annual sports day that engulfs the school for months in preparation. In some of our outstanding schools that have developed a reputation as the most academically demanding in the nation, sports day is the most important event on the school calendar. With students responsible for the event and the long period of preparation leading up to it, the experience of participating in one of the most challenging competitions of their lives leaves an indelible mark on the future leaders of Japan.

The challenge of competition goes beyond the school. During the interviews, so many of the Japanese students framed their answers in relation to America and Americans. To place Japan in perspective, it is invariably America that is applied as the standard for comparison. Often the image of America is distorted. It is not, however, degrading. Most of the students have an ideal image of American society that startles the unsuspecting. As we have seen throughout this study, the Japanese tend to be critical about many aspects of their society. Invariably, perhaps instinctively, they believe the Americans handle similar problems more effectively than the Japanese. If the students are asked a specific question about the notoriously high rates of adult illiteracy in America, for example, they respond knowledgeably, having read about those reports. Still, American education represents to them the ideal, whereas they criticize Japanese education severely. The pervasive grass-looks-greener on the American side remains a critical factor in modern Japanese society.

Regardless of the reality, the ideal perceptions of American society and its institutions held by the future leaders of Japan set a standard for which the Japanese strive. It is a goal that whets their competitive appetite. It motivates them to excel. It drives them to perfectibility. It is a powerful force within the society propelling the Japanese forward in the competition for the future. The leaders of the twenty-first century will reflect a cultural tradition of competitiveness and the challenge of it. And it will be directed at the proverbial catching up with the West, primarily in their ideal image of America.

The challenge of participating in one of the most competitive academic races in the country, through examination preparation for the best universities, and the opportunity to manage the most important sporting event on the school calendar at the top high schools in the land, generates within the future leaders of Japan a basic sense of self-confidence. It rivals that of our Western students in their outstanding schools. The Japanese student is not surrounded with the physical comforts that many of the Western students enjoy, but education in the Oriental tradition is not meant to be enjoyed in comfort. The learner must sacrifice in order to appreciate the learning process. Overcrowded classrooms with fifty students each, in one of the richest nations in the world, is one part necessity and the other part design. To competitively participate successfully, as these students are at the highest level of secondary education in the country, is bound to instill and fortify a basic sense of self-confidence that will serve the future leaders of Japan well.

There is obviously an inconsistency that our students will experience. They have succeeded in the major educational competition of Japan by entering one of the most outstanding high schools in the land. Consequently they realize that their chances of passing the next hurdle of examinations into one of the best universities of the land is decidedly in their favor. There is a degree of self-confidence building among them. And yet when they make comparisons with things Western, or American to most of them, their self-esteem drops. It would seem inevitable that this ambivalence will influence the leaders of Japan in the twenty-first century, as it has in the twentieth century.

There are other characteristics of Japan's outstanding students that illustrate traits worthy of leadership responsibility, domestic or international. A deep distrust of the political excesses of the nation proves vividly that these future leaders are not mindlessly taking notes for examinations. They are quite sophisticated teenagers, in their own somewhat diffident way, harboring profound concerns with the way things are going in their country. They are fairly politically aware and, not infrequently, what they are aware of, they decidedly do not like. Their governmental leaders have been involved in unseemly political activities that have provoked the students' sense of justice and concern for democratic principles. Our survey showed that only 1.5% of the 1,000 Japanese students have much confidence in their political leaders. On the contrary 77% have little confidence in the political leadership of the nation.

A comparison is in order. During the first part of this survey, the American public was absorbed with the so-called Iran scandals, in which the highest public official of the United States, the president, was charged with complicity to circumvent congressional decisions by supplying arms to the Nicaraguan opposition supported by the United States. He denied any knowledge of it. The media convincingly cast strong suspicion on his memory, or lack of it. Subsequently a number of high officials within the White House were judged guilty in court of the very same action, and attempts to conceal it, that they also unequivocally denied under oath. At the very same time high officials of the Japanese government, including the prime minister himself, were criticized for accepting large sums of money for political funding from one company, in return for relatively minor favors that enhanced the financial prospects of the offending company in the innocuous business of employee recruitment. The prime minister resigned to accept responsibility. The American president, in stark contrast, completed his term of office in virtual adulation.

On the identical question of confidence in their government leaders, in which 77% of the future leaders of Japan expressed little confidence, only 26% of the 1,000 future American leaders had little confidence in their political leaders. The results of other questions also showed a disparity between the two groups over trends in their country. Invariably the Japanese were more critical. The political awareness and sensitivity to governmental processes on the part of the future leaders of Japan may indicate a certain sophistication unnoticed in the course of their university examination preparation. They will be as politically sensitive to, pointedly, democratic principles and practices that originated in a Western context as their Western counterparts. Although Americans consider themselves the guardians of democracy, the future leaders of Japan can be expected to be concerned with the principles of democracy and human rights, both of which are practiced in Japan as respectably as in any Western country.

The virtual obsession with interpersonal relationships among the future leaders of Japan, and the society at large, introduces an unusual element into the concept of leadership not always associated with it. The egalitarian nature of Japanese society, in which standing out from the others is not recognized as a virtue, influences the future leaders of Japan in unique ways. First of all, most of the outstanding schools require uniforms that render all students similar in physical appearance, reinforced by the same hair color and facial features. Even though they all know, of course, that they are elite students in elite schools, any hint of their privileged status is disliked. In one of our leading schools, the headmaster on occasion has proudly referred to the special role the students will play in Japan's future, during student assemblies. According to several of them, they react most uncomfortably to it.

Evidence of how this fundamental aspect of Japanese relationships will affect the international community is well under way in the management practices of Japanese-owned companies abroad. For example, the president of another company in this writer's weekly seminar purchased an American company in the greater Boston area, in which the American president was retained. However, the Japanese side soon became disillusioned with him for failing to involve employees up and down the line in the decision-making process, a consensus if you will. The Japanese head office also encouraged him to tear down the walls between staff offices so that all those working in one department place their desks in rows throughout one big open room, common to many Japanese firms. Finally they suggested in vain that the administrative officers take lunch with the other employees in the same cafeteria. After two years of quiet urging, the head office in Japan finally, and most reluctantly, felt compelled to replace their American president. To them, his so-called narrow-minded approach to management and human relations was too removed from the Japanese approach.

To the Japanese, their attitude toward decision making is not simply an attempt to reach a consensus for its own sake. Rather it is considered the most effective method of management in the long run. It may be time-consuming, and in the highly competitive business world, time is money. Nevertheless the participation of many people in the decision-making process tends to induce a feeling of responsibility for the outcome of that decision by those who will implement it. In other words, it is good business to the Japanese. It so happens that it also reflects their social patterns. Their future leaders will make every effort to cultivate these interpersonal relationships whether they become national or international leaders.

As international leaders, the Japanese cannot be expected to provide bold, innovative, imaginative leadership. Their society and its schools, particularly the most outstanding of them, are not designed to encourage or develop those characteristics. Domestically few Japanese leaders can be described as bold, dynamic, and innovative. Curiously many of the companies they manage can be. And that is one of the unique features of Japanese society not fully appreciated outside of it. Without that feature, Japanese industry simply could not compete so effectively in the international marketplace.

The outstanding schools in America and Britain encourage individual initiative and creativity. Their goal is to educate future leaders who someday may develop that elusive charisma that enables one to stand out from another through the force of their personality. The Japanese, on the other hand, are educating their future leaders to be consensus builders and harmonizers. But this does not by any means imply that they do not have new and creative ideas. As individuals, many of them do not. But when they work together with others in a cooperative fashion, impelled by the challenge of their competitors, they rise to the occasion by producing new and innovative ideas that keep their companies highly competitive. For example, *Fortune* (April 9, 1990) reported that "half of Japan's new production capacity in 1990 is being used for products that did not exist five years ago, in an attempt to transform their country into the new-product laboratory for the world, as the U.S. did in the 1950s and 1960s."

Ironically the Japanese have achieved an economic miracle through consensus, an extraordinary accomplishment. That has enabled Japanese industry to compete most effectively with the finest companies in the West, such as IBM where staffers work in their individual offices hopefully creating new and innovative ideas in a very loosely knit team for the next generation of computers. Their Japanese competitors seek the same goal employing, as we have seen, a much different approach. As long as the Japanese approach is successful, there is little reason to induce them to change, that is, to internationalize their methods. Of course there will be fine-tuning, such as sending their people to American universities for MBAs and other advanced degrees that will enable their leaders to adjust to the competition from the West; or the gradual inclusion of more so-called *kikoku shijo*, literally the returning student of families assigned abroad who attended foreign schools learning the local language and customs under natural circumstances. But most of these very same Japanese, upon entering the local work force, as a matter of course will conform pretty well to the traditional behavioral patterns of Japanese society. They are sophisticated enough to understand that those patterns have been very effective in enabling Japan, in spite of its practical and geographical limitations, to become a superpower with new opportunities and responsibilities for the twenty-first century.

There are always a few of the outstanding Japanese students who do not fit comfortably into the system. One within that category is currently a student at this writer's university. A graduate of one of the very elite high schools in our study, he looks and dresses like a 1960-style hippie with long scraggily hair and, to say the least, unusual clothes that stand out amidst a student body that dresses quite stylishly. He most assuredly does not appear as a future leader of Japan on the track to leadership, although he comes from a high school that turns out a good many of them. But once the ice is broken, a clear picture emerges.

Our outstanding student from an outstanding Japanese high school, in fact, hated his school and its academic requirements. And yet while there he started two different clubs for modern dance with a membership of about ten each. In an elite boys' high school, this is an unusually unique accomplishment. The clubs survived his graduation. But the remarkable feature about this misfit, if that is the proper description, is his self-determination to pursue a career in the modern dance field. During his university days he spent most of his time in that pursuit. The dedication to a goal and the determination to meet that challenge engulf his every word. He epitomizes a Japanese seeking perfectibility, but somewhat off the beaten path of mainstream Japan. Beneath the outward appearance of being different lies a sense of self-confidence that matches the most self-confident future leader in our outstanding Western schools. Even though this Japanese student has become interested in a career that is not common in Japan, his chances of achieving his goal, even under extraordinarily difficult circumstances, may be as positive as those with similar ambitions in our Western schools.

We can anticipate from the leaders of Japan in the twenty-first century a degree of dedication and perseverance worthy of a great country. We can also expect a cautious, fairly conservative reaction to new ideas and situations in line with their reaction to the Gulf War. In general, initiatives will not come from the Japanese leaders. Careful responses will, after considerable discussion to arrive at a consensus. There will be those outside the mainstream who appear fresh and daring, un-Japanese, if you please. They may seem unrestricted by Japanese traditions and customs. Underneath appearances, however, tradition exerts its pull, not merely because it is traditional but because the tradition has been so successful. Ultimately realists, the Japanese have followed traditional customs in the modern era since they have proven successful. Otherwise they would have been abandoned long before now, and the outstanding schools that epitomize traditional education, for example, would have been drastically reformed.

International leaders from other countries will, to some degree, simply have to adjust to the Japanese ways of leadership since their financial power enables them to take liberties never possible before. A similar situation took place in the early part of the twentieth century when the Americans, then a second-class nation, burst on to the international scene with their brash manners and nonconforming ideas. The Europeans had to adjust to the new order since the Americans from the "new world" had accumulated the financial, and later military, power to back up their policies.

In a similar way the Japanese are now in a position to exert global influence in their own manner in the twenty-first century. The major difference is that the Japanese, as we have seen in this study, are ever-mindful of their small country conspicuously devoid of natural resources existing among world leaders. Appropriately their conduct is governed by caution, perhaps modesty, as one should with a fragile foundation. The Americans throughout most of this century believed in the inevitability of global leadership, with their large and powerful nation leading mankind into a new world, and acted accordingly. The Japanese are in no position to enjoy such luxuries.

There are both similarities and differences between the Americans in the early twentieth century and the Japanese in the twenty-first century. The Americans had their eye on the future, on a new world order, and were anxious to discard all trappings of the old European traditions. Change was the order of the day. For example, the classic study of the transition of American schools from the European patterns that were brought to America in the eighteenth and nineteenth centuries into the new American school for the twentieth century was appropriately titled *The Transformation of the School*, authored by the late great teacher Laurence Cremin, mentioned in the Dedication of this book, whose lectures remain so vivid to those of us who took his courses. It was indeed a revolution of the classroom, the role of the teacher, and virtually every other facet of the school in the transformation of a traditional school into the progressive school designed for the future.

At the center of the new education was the child-centered classroom replacing the traditional subject-centered classroom, as envisioned by John Dewey and the progressive education movement. Even the name of the movement presaged the twentieth century as the American Century, in which American individualism, an outgrowth of the frontier, formed the basis of their new progressive world. That, in turn, would be projected on a global scale so that American progressivism would lead mankind into the new era of American democracy. America fever excited the world. In other words, the American Century of the 1900s was launched with a transformation of its schools.

In one of the truly unique twists in modern history, the Americans had the opportunity to project their revolutionary concepts in education onto Japan during the postwar American Occupation. In an attempt to democratize Japanese society and its institutions in the American image, they set out to reconstruct the schools. Embodied in the Fundamental Law of Education of 1947, sanctioned if not written by the American authorities, the focus was placed squarely on the development of individualism accordingly: "We shall esteem individual dignity . . . (with education) rich in individuality. Education shall aim at the full development of personality . . . and be imbued with the independent spirit."

Maintaining total control over occupied Japan, General MacArthur's military government proceeded to dismantle the traditional Japanese school system controlled by the Ministry of Education. The classroom was a major target of the American reformers. The report of the U.S. Education Mission to Japan in 1946 struck at the very heart of the Japanese school: "Teaching methods emphasizing memorization, conformity, and a vertical system of duties and loyalties should be modified to encourage independent thinking, the development of personality, and the rights and responsiblities of democratic citizenship. . . . Knowledge must be acquired that is broader than any available in a single prescribed textbook or manual, and deeper than can be tested by stereotyped examinations."

The American approach to teaching and learning never really caught on in Japan. It was unnatural. It fit the American experience more appropriately than it fit Japanese customs and behavior. The Japanese turned away from it as soon as possible. In fact the reform of the classroom envisioning an interaction between the student and teacher, with the student at the center of the learning process in an effort to develop independent thinking, was simply too radical for the average Japanese teacher to manage from the very beginning. Tradition proved too powerful a sanction of the central role of examination preparation in the classroom. In a word, the American Occupation reforms of postwar Japanese education did not basically alter the traditional approach to the teaching-learning process in the classroom. It persists to this very day in our outstanding schools educating far more than their share of Japan's future leaders. Speculation leads one to wonder if Japan would have become an economic superpower if the American Occupation reforms of the Japanese classroom had been effectively implemented.

The transition of Japan from a second-class power into a superpower at the turn of the twenty-first century must necessarily follow a different path than that of the Americans at the beginning of this century. Their leaders must accordingly be judged by different criteria. Japanese leadership reflects Japanese society with its deep historical roots in an Oriental context, just as the American leadership of the twentieth century mirrored an America profoundly influenced by its brief experience as a frontier society. The major difference in the American and Japanese paths into world leadership is that Japan, from all indications, will not transform its schools from the traditional into the progressive for the twenty-first century.

The future leaders of Japan, then, are experiencing a school tradition that has not undergone any fundamental change in order to prepare them for a new role in the next century. Consequently we cannot anticipate bold and decisive leaders who inspire others to greatness. Rather we can expect Japan's future leaders at home and abroad to act prudently, patiently, and modestly, precisely how they responded in this survey. It reflects Japanese society. So, too, will the Japanese leaders of the twenty-first century.

INDEX

ABOUT THE AUTHOR

BENJAMIN C. DUKE is Chairman of the Graduate Faculty of Education, Director of American Studies, and Professor of Comparative and International Education at the International Christian University in Tokyo where he has been teaching for the past 30 years. Before that he was a public school teacher in the United States.

Professor Duke's research and teaching has concentrated on education in Asia. One of his works, *The Japanese School*, a study of the impact of Japanese schools on Japan's post–World War II economic development, was published in both English (Praeger, 1986) and Japanese. His other publications, *Ten Great Educators from Modern Japan*, *Japan's Militant Teachers: A History of the Left Wing Teachers Movement*, *The Karachi Plan: Master Design for Education in Asia*, "Democratic Education: Divergent Patterns in Japan and America," and "Why Noriko Can Read: Some Hints for Johnny" reflect his various studies of both Japanese and comparative education.